HOW to FEED the MEDIAVORE

Also by Heather Thompson Day:
Cracked Glasses
Hook, Line, and Sinker

To order, call **1-800-765-6955.**
Visit us at **www.reviewandherald.com** for information on other
Review and Herald® products.

To contact Heather to speak at your church or school, send an e-mail to:
AuthorHeatherMarie@aol.com.

HEATHER THOMPSON DAY

HOW to FEED the MEDIAVORE

THE
30-DAY
CHALLENGE

REVIEW AND HERALD® PUBLISHING ASSOCIATION
Since 1861 | www.reviewandherald.com

Published by Review and Herald® Publishing Association, Hagerstown, MD 21741-1119

Review and Herald® titles may be purchased in bulk for educational, business, fund-raising, or sales promotional use. For information, e-mail SpecialMarkets@reviewandherald.com.

The Review and Herald® Publishing Association publishes biblically based materials for spiritual, physical, and mental growth and Christian discipleship.

The author assumes full responsibility for the accuracy of all facts and quotations as cited in this book.

Bible texts in this book are from the *Holy Bible, New International Version.* Copyright © 1973, 1978, 1984, 2011 by Biblica, Inc. Used by permission. All rights reserved worldwide.

Statements in this book attributed to other speakers/writers are included for the value of the individual statements only. No endorsement of those speakers'/writers' other works or statements is intended or implied.

This book was
Edited by Megan Mason
Copyedited by Delma Miller
Cover designed by Daniel Anez / Review and Herald® Design Center
Cover photo by © Thinkstock.com
Interior designed by Emily Ford / Review and Herald® Design Center
Typeset: Minion Pro 11/13

PRINTED IN U.S.A.

17 16 15 14 13   5 4 3 2 1

Library of Congress Cataloging-in-Publication Data

Day, Heather Thompson
  How to feed the mediavore : the 30-day challenge / Heather Thompson Day.
    pages cm
  ISBN 978-0-8280-2635-2
  1. Spirituality. 2. Spiritual
life--Christianity. 3. Social media. I. Title.
  BV4501.3.T47255 2014
  241'.65--dc23
                          2012049325

ISBN 978-0-8280-2635-2

Dedication

I am dedicating this book to the cutest boy in my sixth-grade class, **Seth Michael Day,** who later became my husband, and to a little girl who has given me a glimpse of how Christ must feel, **London Marie Day.** I love you both so intensely that if I let myself think about it too much, I quite literally feel as if my heart will explode. Thank you for breathing a new kind of passion into my life.

Forever and always,
Heather

Dear Reader,

I read the *Hunger Games* trilogy in about two weeks. That's 400 pages each book, give or take. Nielsen ratings from 2010 showed that that year the average American watched 34 hours of television each week. When you compare this with the notion that a typical full-time job is 40 hours a week, you are just a few episodes shy of a career. People spend more than 700 billion minutes per month on Facebook, and the Entertainment Software Association reported that 72 percent of American families play video games.

One of the characteristics of our generation is that we are *mediavores*. We eat, sleep, and breathe media. We consume it without even thinking. The media is setting the standard for how we think and feel, and I am beginning to worry about how we can spiritually feed a generation that is already full. I don't claim to know all the answers, but I do agree with my husband, who has pointed out that we humans seem to keep asking God to help us create time for Him in the midst of everything else when we should be asking how to create time for everything else in the midst of what we are doing for Him.

I believe beyond a shadow of a doubt that Christ is preparing to flip this world upside down. A time is coming when the call will be made for the just to remain just, and for the unjust to remain unjust (Revelation 22:11). We have absolutely no clue what we are about to find ourselves getting into, but I do know that we simply won't survive a minute of it if we don't cling tight to the feet of our Savior. Jesus, the one whom they called Christ, is asking you to reprioritize your schedule. He wants to spend some time with you. Jesus needs you to connect with Him in order to be saved, and I'm sorry, but there is not an app for that.

Take the 30-Day Challenge!

—Heather Thompson Day

Day 1

Growing up in today's world is hard. Growing up a Christian in today's world is even harder. In between gaming entertainment such as Call of Duty, movies and television propaganda, and keeping up with all your social ties on all the social networks, life can be downright exhausting. School and homework, girlfriends and boyfriends, parties and texting—it can really be hard to find a moment to sit down and devote any time to honing your relationship with God, even if you know you need to. Life in this tech-savvy era that we are now living in makes it hard to be unconnected enough from the world to find any time to connect with God.

This semester I had to take a few more religious prerequisites before starting my doctoral program. I am currently enrolled in a class at the seminary called Ministry to Youth and Young Adults, taught by Allan Walshe. We spend a great deal of our time in this class discussing this young adult, or millennial, generation. He provided us with several characteristics that depict millennials, one of which is that they/we are mediavores. By this he meant that we are literally surrounded by media. We consume it without thinking. We relax with it, entertain with it, aimlessly sift through it; and just about every time I meet with my students, I find a way to teach with it. We are literally being spoon-fed all of our information by the media, and we are stuffed. So my question became How do you spiritually feed a mediavore who is already stuffed full of secular information?

I'm not here to argue whether you should watch TV, play video games, or spend two hours of your day stalking your exes on Facebook. I will tell you that I am 24 years old, and after doing my M.A. research project on the role of Facebook in our romantic relationships, I learned enough to know I needed to shut it down. But then I got pregnant, and the comments came rolling in that our family in different states needed us to create a Facebook page so that we could stay connected. We obliged, and my husband and I created an account together, which we use to share photos of our daughter. How families stayed connected before social media, I'll never know. Do you think they actually phoned each other? The point is, we practically can't escape it. We are being overindulged, and cutting the fat is trickier than one might think.

This generation, unlike any generation before, is growing up wireless, and it has radically changed not only our communication but also our relationships. Performics Today did a study in 2010 surveying more than 3,000 respondents. They found that 51 percent of people say social sites are the best way to communicate with friends and family. It may be extreme to say that social media has replaced our relationships, but you could certainly claim that it is reinventing the way we do them. For the first time in earth's history, more people are communicating with their family and friends through social media than face-to-face interaction.

What are the biggest implications social media has had on our lives? The biggest is TMI (too much information). Suddenly, the only thing we know about privacy is that it is in our control settings. Many of us tend to be much more revealing in business and personal communications than ever before. Somehow, telling the world personal things and then exploring them on our blogs, on Facebook, and on Twitter has become socially acceptable in many circles. How many times have you seen a status or tweet about someone's sex life, embarrassing moment, or personal family drama? It seems as though nothing is off-limits anymore. Anything goes!

Our generation has now grown up virtually. What happens when you grow up online, in an age with TMI? The *Journal of Adolescent Research* did a study following the blogs of adolescent girls. Adolescent girls have emerged as the largest demographic of bloggers in the United States. The researcher did a case study looking at 20 girls, ages 17-21, who had been blogging for three or more years.

The author, Katie Davis, said this: "Those of us who recall our own teenage diaries, guarded with lock and key beneath our beds, may marvel at this new, public form of journaling. As youths' enthusiasm for blogging grows, many of the adults in their lives worry that such online self-disclosure will lead to victimization at the hands of peer bullies or adult predators."

Not only are we providing deeper levels of self-disclosure for anyone to see; we are also becoming addicted to it. Suddenly you have a stage where everyone who comes to your page is coming to see and hear about you. You get to be a mini-celebrity, and we are fooling ourselves if we think narcissism isn't going to take a toll on our spiritual lives. Christianity is all about minimizing the self and glorifying Christ. Social media tends to put a lot of emphasis on glorifying yourself, and most of the time it's unintentional.

So how do you feed a mediavore? All I want you to do is to take 30 days to connect with God as though He was actually one of your friends. Take 30 days out of 365 and spend about 15 minutes out of each day to commune with God. I should note that I have a friend in the seminary who committed to doing a media fast. At the end of his two weeks he posted a status on Facebook that said something along the lines of "I've learned that even if you stay away from the media, if you don't make a choice to spend that extra time connecting with Christ you will just fill it doing something else." His statement is true. There is no easy fix here. Diets are always hard, and it won't work without commitment.

George Barna of the Barna group recently did a study looking at the reason young people are leaving the church. We are looking at some drear statistics here when we look at the present state of our church community. Research has shown that 60 percent of young people are leaving the church. Sixty percent! The youth of our churches are emptying their pews. These vibrant souls with the innovative ideas, the up-and-coming future leaders with new ways of thinking, the young, unbridled, and fresh members of our church communities, are vanishing at numbers as high as six out of every 10. That is not meant to sound so third person—I am talking about us; I am talking about you. If the trees are fading away and the seeds they planted are being uprooted at alarming speeds, how long will it take for the orchard to disappear completely?

Barna's five-year study was put into a book by David Kinnaman called *You Lost Me: Why Young Christians Are Leaving Church . . . and Rethinking Church.* In one article Kinnaman deduces six reasons for what happens to youth in regards to their church life after the age of 15. Some of the various reasons are that they feel church is too stifling, it is too shallow, it doesn't match with what they understand to be true according to science, and they feel that Christianity is too exclusive in a very inclusive America. By exclusive they are referring to the list of things church says that you should not do, which I suppose could make those who want to continue doing those things feel excluded. The last reason cited is that the church simply seems unfriendly to those who may have doubts.

What I think is interesting, though, is that in spite of all this, another characteristic of this millennial generation is that we are hungry for spirituality, and we are hungry for community. So there it is: the mixed bag of bad and good news. Prof. Walshe made a statement to our classroom that I am going to make to you right now before we go any further. He said, "It is up to you to start the change." His favorite line to inspire us with is "You are God's next big thing." I don't think he was just talking to my classroom when he said that, or even just to me. I think he was being a bit more inclusive than that. I think what he meant to say was You, right there reading this book right now—you're also God's next big thing.

I had a realization yesterday, and I talked it over with my husband last evening. I realized that I believe in God, and because of that belief, I make an effort to spend time with Him every morning. You see, I believe that He exists, and so for the past few years, every morning I wake up, read my Bible, read a devotional, pray, and then I'm out the door. I have been doing this for years, and I was feeling really good about myself. Yesterday, however, something struck me.

I believe in Jesus as the Creator of the universe. I believe He is the sustainer of my life, and because of that, I petition Him every day to use me. I believe that this entire world, and every year I am alive, is meant to serve as nothing more than my preparation for His kingdom. I acknowledge Him as the sole reason for my existence, and yet I was only giving Him 25-30 minutes of my day, and it felt good. If God is who He says He is, and my role in life is simply to use my gifts and talents to bring Him glory, then I have been severely disconnected. My husband put it this way: "Isn't it funny that we spend so much time trying to get the best job with the most money, the best car, and the biggest house, and really at the end of the day, the only thing we will take to heaven is our relationship with Christ and the seeds we planted in others?"

It was his making that statement that pulled me out of my Ph.D. in communications program in Virginia and landed me a seat at Andrews University. I started registering for electives in the Religion Department. Don't get me wrong: I love studying communications, but I knew that if I was going to join the 1 percent of Americans with a Ph.D. and pour in the countless hours of reading and writing, I wanted to also do it while studying and learning more about my beautiful Savior. I couldn't keep writing Christian books without taking a moment to study that same Christ academically. My experience in those classes has left me forever changed. You see, my husband's right—my academic awards and my degrees aren't going to heaven with me, but my relationship with Jesus, and the seeds I plant from here on out, will.

I think part of our disconnection occurs because it is so easy to be stimulated in this world. When my mom was young, she probably had four or five really good girlfriends. Now the average Facebook user has 134. It's not that this society is not all about forming relationships and maintaining bonds; we are busier than ever connecting with people. So busy that perhaps we have started to leave out the only Person who actually matters.

This generation is hungry for community and spirituality. When I found this out, I made it a point not only to continue in my own personal daily devotions, but also to form a Bible study. It's a small group of us. We meet once a week for an hour to an hour and a half, and we explore the Word of God through this powerful tool called community. My husband and I are the only Adventists, but we are always accepting new members. The group is comprised of nondenominational young people, a Baptist, and us. We've had arguments and heated debates, but at the end of the day all of us are desperate for a further understanding of Jesus Christ, and that's what keeps us coming back for more.

I would venture to say that many young adults are leaving church after the age of 15, not because there were no other fellow believers, but perhaps, because of a lack of authenticity. It is hard to be a Christian. Trust me: if anyone understands the struggle of imperfection, I think it is safe to raise my hand first. But if my peers are looking for an authentic relationship with Christ, I can't think of a better church for them to be witnessing that in.

The Adventist Church has a great deal of information, and I think that is a pillar we can be proud of. What we may not be quite as good at, which may be another reason we are seeing young people who are thirsty for community, is maintaining relationships. I shared this thought with Battle Creek Academy during their Bible camp, at which my husband and I were the presenters. During their Sabbath school program the principal asked a question regarding where their favorite place to worship was. He had them text in their answers. They were able to choose from a few different things—a park bench, the beach, alone in my room, or at church. Not one person in this roomful of high school students paying for private education texted in the response of church. They would rather worship God anywhere else but church. I jotted that detail down, and when I got up to speak I mentioned it to them. I told them that this said more to me about the state of our church's youth programs than it did about them. We have got to be building community in our churches. What I meant by that was that *you* have got to start building community in your church. After all, you are God's next big thing.

I decided that I couldn't sit back and write another word if I didn't start the change with me, and so in an effort to build a bit of community I started a Bible study, and it has been incredibly fulfilling. Like me, you also are probably full of church doctrine, biblical knowledge, and have a pretty good foundation of what is needed for salvation. You also probably have the information part of this thing down, and that is great, but how are you doing with building authentic Christian relationships?

I have more gay friends than I have fingers. I used to work for a major brand-name label clothing company as their store manager. I left with more than just a few extra outfits; I also left with incredible friendships. I had lunch with a friend of mine the other week who is a homosexual. My gay friend is the sweetest, most thoughtful individual I have ever met. I can honestly say I love him and that he has been nothing but attentive in our friendship. He calls me on my birthday, buys me books, and listens when I need to vent. He is a wonderful man, and is terribly confused as he struggles with his sexual desires. After we ate and shot the breeze, his face turned a little more serious.

"Heather, what do you think about my sexuality?" he said.

I thought perhaps this conversation might come up, though I didn't really want it to. I know this isn't right, but, if I am being completely honest, I can admit that up until this point I was enjoying dodging and evading this very conversation. As I said before, I am far from perfect, and I certainly didn't think it was my place to start lecturing him on the life choices he was making. That's the sad thing about sin: it's hard to be candid with someone else, even your friends, when Satan is so articulate with the speeches he whispers into your thoughts, reminding you of the past you've desperately been trying to make up for. Too many skeletons can make even clear lines seem blurry.

I did, however, feel an obligation to provide him with honest feedback if he should ever directly ask me for my opinion. I gulped a bit of air down my already-dry throat and mumbled a quick prayer in my head that God would provide me with the right words on such a delicate issue. After all, a few wrong ones here, and he may decide he didn't want to be my friend anymore, an option that would have wounded me greatly.

"Do you think I can ever be happy? Or do you think I have to spend the rest of my life alone, and just get a dog?"

I didn't want to hurt his feelings, and I honestly thought for a moment about telling him what he wanted to hear. I then thought about our friendship, about the kindness that he had shown to me in the past, and I decided I had to be kind and honest in respect to our friendship now.

"Well," I began, "I believe that you really do have those feelings." I wanted first to validate that I understood that this actually was an issue for him. I didn't want him to think that I couldn't see how emotionally torn up he seemed about this.

"I believe you that it is hard and that there is probably a war going on in your heart. I am also your friend, and though part of me really wants to tell you what I know you want to hear, it wouldn't make me a good friend." He caught my eyes now and wrestled them into submission to his.

"The truth is," I continued, "I know that society is busy telling you—and me, for that matter—that we have only one life to live, so make it count. Your other friends are probably screaming for you to seize the moment, live every day as if it is your last! But the truth is that, in my opinion, Satan is feeding us lies. You do have more than one life to live, and this one won't even scratch the surface. If you compare the 80 years we may live on this planet to even the thousand years we will spend with God in heaven before even coming to live for eternity in the new earth, there is simply no comparison. It would be foolish to allow our desires in this life, sexual or otherwise, to hinder our salvation. Heaven will be where life begins, and to miss out on that to have a good time for 80 years here is not only foolish—it is exactly how naive Satan is hoping we will be."

His face finally fell. It was not the answer he wanted to hear. As we sat there longer, a few of those moments in silence, he thoughtfully told me that he had never really looked at things that way. He thanked me for providing a different view from the one his other friends had been telling him. He said he needed to hear it, even if he didn't want to. Now, I don't know what he will choose in the end. I told him I would pray for him, and I can honestly say that I do. The point of this story wasn't to discuss my philosophy on homosexuality. My opinion may not be your opinion, and I'm OK with that if you are.

My point, however, is that whatever our desires are, whether sexually immoral or for vanity, anything that has the potential to separate us from eternal life with God is not worth it. Maybe for you it is alcohol, or drugs, or heterosexual sex outside of marriage, or your boyfriend or girlfriend, or Facebook, or vanity, or an obsession with celebrities. Whatever it is that is keeping you from coming to God with your whole heart is simply not worth it.

Sometimes it's not even our present that hinders us from coming to God completely, but our past. As I said earlier, Satan is really good at recycling old laundry. For a long time what kept me from completely connecting with Christ was not what I was doing, but what I had done. Guilt is probably still my biggest struggle. It's hard for me, if I let myself think too long about who I've been, to accept the person God is now calling me to be. Satan has one strategy in mind when it comes to God and us: separation.

If guilt is the ticket to keeping you from Christ's feet, Satan will make sure you have a never-ending supply of it. If it's sex, money, alcohol, pornography, or anger that causes a divide between your path and the cross, expect to somehow see these things start popping up even in unexpected places. You see, Satan, probably more than anyone, knows that the key to salvation is connection, and so separation is always his game plan, and the ends always justify the means.

Jesus said in Matthew 5:30, "If your right hand causes you to stumble, cut it off and throw it away. It is better for you to lose one part of your body than for your whole body to go into hell." Here we see Him being symbolic, but in some ways also literal. I think what He was getting at is that nothing is worth losing eternity. If anyone can attest to the glories of heaven, it is He.

I have had sins that I knew hindered my prayers. It wasn't easy, but I had to start cutting things out of my life that I knew were only hurting me; and to be honest, I'm still cutting. I may be writing devotionals now, but I promise I am still a work in progress. This is not me preaching from my high horse. This is simply writings from one friend who's been there to another.

First Timothy 1:15 sums up my life completely, saying, "Christ Jesus came into the world to save sinners—of whom I am the worst."

I love that verse. Christ Jesus came into the world to save sinners! Only a person who is afflicted with guilt can really appreciate this verse. I want to savor every word. When Christ was creating the salvation plan, when the Trinity was meeting to discuss the pros and cons of even creating this creature called man, who They knew would fall, Jesus decided to move forward with the ultimate gift of the Crucifixion in order to save the sinner. Not the righteous, not the holy, not the perfect or the pious. He allowed Himself to be born into this pathetic race called humanity for sinners, for me.

We may be weak and ugly and small, but we are exactly who Christ came into this world looking to save. It's not as though He came to earth and then said, "Oh, man, if I'd known who was down here, I would never have come."

On the contrary, we are exactly what He hoped to find: people in need of grace, which He freely gives. Satan spends every waking moment on this strategy called separation. God's already signed, sealed, and delivered the greatest gift you'll ever receive; and Satan is methodically hoping he can persuade you into either picking up something else or leaving the wrapping untorn because, like me, you are unsure if something so beautiful could really have your name printed on it. This life is like cubic zirconia. It's second-rate, it's cheap, it's a look-alike, a fraud; and everyone's trying to convince you that this shine is as good as it gets, so you might as well lose yourself in it. Trust me: the best is yet to come. Out of the pressure of the fiercest coals will come the most beautiful diamonds.

The gift has already been bought, the package has already been wrapped, and there's no mistaking that that is your name written in bold. This is no time for pleasantries. Like a child literally salivating, hungry for the biggest gift under the tree, we need to rip that box open without any concern for the wrapping, and allow ourselves to grab hold of that extended hand and feel nothing but pure, naked connection.

Consider the next 30 days as a giant pair of scissors. Let's start trimming the fat that keeps us hiding from Him in shame. Let's reconnect with an old friend. Christ may not have a social network in which you can post on His wall, but He did have a cross; and I can assure you that right in this moment He is begging you to post your thoughts, worries, praise, and guilt right to those beams.

Reflection: "Cast your cares on the Lord and he will sustain you" (Psalm 55:22).

Day 2

"There is a big world out there . . . bigger than prom, bigger than high school, and it won't matter if you were the prom queen, the quarterback of the football team, or the biggest nerd in school. Find out who you are and try to not be afraid of it."
—Josie Geller (Drew Barrymore), in the movie *Never Been Kissed*

When I was 8 years old, my mother was the most beautiful woman in my world. She had this perfect dirty-blond hair and these incredible sharp green eyes. Sometime that year I had found a picture of her when she was a teenager. It was the later part of the 1970s, and she was wearing black leather pants and a white blouse. She was standing next to her best friend, who was equally as striking. I took that picture and hid it in my room as if it were some kind of secret treasure that was only mine.

I used to watch her get ready in the mornings. My mother was still the woman in my hidden picture, only now she had traded her leather pants for dress skirts. I wondered if she had hidden those black leather pants somewhere deep in her closet, just as I had hidden that photo. I kept the photo for years and burned a mental image of it into my mind, all the while hoping and praying that that image was a direct look into my future. Perhaps if I held my breath long enough or wished hard enough, I'd one day sprout into that girl whose sparkling smile was trapped in the image. I'd trade my ordinary curly brown hair for her straight blond hair, and my dull brown eyes for a pair of captivating green. In my few moments of solace I'd sit in the bathroom and stare at myself in the mirror. I'd dip into her reddest lipstick and try to brush it on delicately. I'd purse my lips and kiss the air, imagining I was the girl in that photo.

When I was 14, I entered high school. I was terrified to be seen, and equally as scared to go unnoticed. Many of the other girls became women over the summer. Their bodies were suddenly flawless, and they had acquired an aura about them that spoke through the silence that they had grown up. I was still as shapeless and skinny as I was in middle school, and the only thing my aura whispered was that I was invisible.

I don't mean to throw a pity party. I am sure that there were girls there who felt worse off than I did. There is one thing I have learned in my life, and that is that perception is reality. It doesn't really matter how others view you; all that matters is how you view yourself. Your perception is your reality. Change your perception, change reality.

The first day of high school a few of my girlfriends got dropped off at my house. The thought of entering that giant school solo was scarier than a horror film. We had no idea what would meet us through those doors, and though we were anxious to find out, we believed in strength in numbers. Of all the scary things that would be lurking around the high school walls, boys seemed the scariest. It was hard enough being noticed by the boys in my own class. Now I was being thrown into a school with what felt like a million other girls, many of them older than me, and probably better looking.

Before school started, my best friend at the time and I would sit in her room talking about the junior and senior boys we would soon be in school with.

"Do you think they'll ever talk to us?" I'd ask her.

She was beautiful. Tracy knew how to get noticed. She was that girl in middle school all the boys wanted to date and all the girls wanted to be. I got to be that girl's best friend, which can be both wonderful and a hard position to be in at 13 years old. Sometimes you want someone to know your name because it matters, not just because they want to ask you if Tracy noticed them that day.

"Of course they will!" she answered, almost confused I would even pose the question. She had sharp green eyes too, and platinum blond hair, much like the beautiful woman in the photo I had hidden. Those girls weren't afraid of big buildings, older girls, or new boys; those girls didn't have to be.

Looking back, I am still not sure where exactly I did fit in in the scheme of high school. In my mind I feel that I was kind of always good, but never good enough. I'd get voted onto the homecoming court, but of course would never win. I hung out with popular kids, but I was never the belle of any ball. Not to mention there are aspects of my personality that were quite honestly geeky. I love to read, and I clearly love to write. The second they let me, I entered journalism class and became an editor on the school paper. Typically the cool kids weren't reading teenage novels or trying to get interviews with the superintendent for a journalism story. I don't think they even read the school paper. I was just different.

I remember, for example, spending a great deal of time and energy writing an editorial piece on how there was no box to check for biracial children. You know how when you apply for various things they ask you to check your race? Well, you could check either Black or White, and for those of us who were both, you had to decide which parent you wanted to identify with. This was not OK with me. I feel very connected and attached to both of my parents, and therefore feel that same level of connectedness toward my biracial identity. I was not going to pick just one race, because I am not just one race. I interviewed the principal, who said the superintendent made the form. When I called the superintendent, he sent me back to the principal. I was in circles. When I finally printed the article, feeling very happy with my work, a few kids made fun of me for it.

"Who cares, Thompson?" they asked while laughing. For the rest of high school my nickname was Oprah Winfrey.

They didn't get it, and I didn't care. That same article later placed third at the Michigan Interscholastic Press Association out of 1,500 applicants. Validation is a wonderful feeling, but not if you are the only person in the school that even knows or cares about the Michigan Interscholastic Press Association. I was trying to raise awareness about a problem, and my friends just thought I was a weirdo.

I was madly in love with Rocky Boswell, a boy in my class and star athlete. He was kind enough to share with me all the girls he was madly in love with, none of which ever happened to be me.

"You're my best friend, Thompson," he'd say, as if that were to be some sort of compliment. I'd still kept that picture hidden in my room, and I knew that if I had just been that girl in the photo, then everything could be different.

Throughout high school I remained Rocky's best friend. In those four years I am pretty sure he dated every single girl I was friends with, acquaintances with, or even noticed, but he never dated me. There were times he spent weeks trying to get the nerve up to ask Tracy on a date, and who do you think was right there forcing a smile? That's right, Oprah Winfrey. I'm pretty sure Tracy knew how I felt about Rocky, but that didn't stop her from hanging out with him either.

"Are you sure you don't mind?" she'd ask me out of politeness.

"Of course not," I'd respond while gritting my teeth.

The only thing worse than not being noticed would have been to become noticed as the only roadblock in someone else's teen romance. The last thing I needed was to receive hate mail from Rocky because he saw me as the thorn in his side that prevented things from progressing with Tracy. I'd rather smile and wave while holding on to Tracy's coattails. Sometimes you hear stories like this and you are waiting for the rainbow after the storm, the cute and happy ending that ties it all together. I have no happy ending to this story for you. It wasn't fun, I wasn't always happy, and there were many nights I cried myself to sleep. The happy ending is to thank God that high school is only four years long and that everyone eventually moves on. Let's hope you'll do bigger things with your life than be crowned prom queen.

If I'm being honest, there are still moments I feel as if I am 8 or 14 years old, watching from the sidelines, invisible, as life happens for everyone else. There have been times I still swap my emotions of jealousy for a fake happiness because someone got the great job I wish I'd had or the big car or the nice house.

It's a sick and twisted monster that lives somewhere deep inside me that makes me believe that no matter what I do, I'll always be good, but never be good enough. As Christians we often spend a lot of time and effort trying to convince ourselves to have faith in God. I feel as though we have it all backwards. Faith in God is easy. God is perfection. He is beautiful, holy, all-powerful, and all-knowing. God is the measuring stick to which it seems you'll never measure up.

He is good, has always been good, and will always be good. He's that star athlete in every small-town high school, that girl with the flawless figure, or the woman in the picture you know you'll never be. He's perfect, and that's where the chasm between Him and us comes into play, because He is everything we're not. It's hard to build a relationship or feel anything but invisible to someone who is so far out of our league. Faith in Him is easy. It's putting faith into ourselves, faith into the idea that we are somebody who has something to offer this world, that can be hard.

At least, in my experience, it's been difficult to put faith in myself and the plan He has for me, and so I blow it.

Surely He isn't looking at me, I think to myself. It's funny, but in a way it's kind of like all of life is like your first year of high school. But here's the thing: If the most popular kid in school calls you by name and tells you that they saved a seat for you at lunch, you don't argue with them that you're a loser and that that seat should go to someone cooler. You seize the chance and jump on your opportunity to reverse your invisibility. You sit in that seat and spend the rest of the year holding your head up a little higher because you've just been noticed.

As insignificant as you may feel, God has already noticed you. He selected you and called you from your mother's womb. He gave you life, has blessed you with years to live it, and even the fact that you are reading these words proves that He is trying desperately to get your attention. Jesus Christ, the one being who is fully God and fully man, has already spotted you and knows you by name. He knows your name, not because you were or weren't prom queen, not because you did or did not get that promotion, and not because your best friend is Tracy. He knows your name because in you He sees something incredibly special.

God, the Bright and Morning Star of the universe, thinks you are a big deal. He's got a seat saved just for you at His table. We have to stop watching life happen for everyone else and get out there and seize our moment to be someone. Put some faith into yourself, because there really is no mistaking it: He's looking right at you. So how are you going to use this incredible opportunity?

Reflection: "But you are a chosen people, a royal priesthood, a holy nation, God's special possession, that you may declare the praises of him who called you out of darkness into his wonderful light" (1 Peter 2:9).

Day 3

"Growing up is never easy. You hold on to things that were;
you wonder what's to come. But that night, I think we knew it was time
to let go of what had been, and look ahead to what would be—other
days, new days, days to come. The thing is we didn't have to hate each
other for getting older; we just had to forgive ourselves for growing up."

—Kevin Arnold, the narrator (Daniel Stern) in the TV show *The Wonder Years*

If I'd had things my way, I'd be a recording artist by now. You always hear those stories of the child-prodigy-turned-superstar who came out of the womb singing. Everyone spots an entertainer almost instantly. They're that kid who just has some contagious spark when they sing, even though they aren't really sure what to do with it all yet. In my mind I was that kid. The first thing I ever wrote was a song. I remembered that song on my drive to work the other day, and I still knew every word.

I had an exceptional childhood. I had these incredibly adoring but honest parents, and my big sister, unlike most big sisters, made me feel so cool. She thought I had "it," I could tell. She was three years older than I was, but she took me everywhere and laughed at all my material. To this day she's a woman of very few loving words, but she's filled to the brim with precious actions. I was her favorite person, and though she never said it, she also never had to.

I honestly think the biggest contributing factor to my becoming who I am is the people God put on this earth to raise me and love me. When the world didn't always get me, I had so many loving arms to run into. I may have battled normal girl insecurities, but I always knew where I stood with my family. I always knew that I had a spot where I fit in perfectly, and it made all the difference.

At any rate, I can remember spending countless hours writing music in my bedroom. I loved to sing. It gave me more than just a tangible voice; it provided me with a creative outlet. My dad had lived a successful career on Broadway, and I didn't just want to follow in his footsteps; I wanted to be better than he ever was. I wanted to make my own magic.

My father and I have always been incredibly close. You know how in life everyone has that one person, and even though the whole world can tell you that you did excellent at something, but if you don't hear that from them, none of it matters? On the same hand, the whole world could tell you that you stink, but if that one person looks you in the eye and says they're wrong, you believe them. My father is that person for me. He's the first man I ever loved, and even now as an adult I feel incredibly lucky to have had the relationship with him that I did.

They say the first five years of a child's life are actually the most crucial to their development. Research suggests that this is when we develop our "love map," our understanding of how to give and receive love. If a child suffers a tragedy after the first five years, they can overcome it, but if the tragedy is suffered during the first five years of life it's incredibly challenging to have a normal, healthy adulthood. The first five years of my life were spent mostly with my father. He worked and traveled a lot, doing evangelism ministry, but he was also the one who watched me all day and took me to preschool. I am pretty sure that it is because of these first five years that we spent together that I have this incredible bond with him, deeper than most father-daughter relationships.

So many young girls don't have dads that made them feel dearly cherished as children. His love and affection toward me pushed me to demand the same (if not more) love and affection in a mate. My father taught me that I was special, and I believed him. What a different race of women we would have if every man took his job as father to a tiny baby girl as seriously as mine did. It's incredibly important to the psyche as those little girls grow and become strong women.

I always tell my husband that he can be certain of a few things with our daughter. She will never outgrow needing to hear him tell her she's beautiful. She will always, regardless of her attitude, secretly think he is the smartest man in the world. And at some point, in between 2 and 5, she will probably ask him to marry her.

"Sweetheart," my daddy said to me one day when I was 6 or 7 years old and on the brink of a musical career, "you can't sing." He gave it to me straight. "Your songs are very cute, though. Polish those; use your gifts!" And then he walked away.

I wouldn't say I was devastated. I was, and still am for the most part, pretty resilient. I was shocked if anything, because I really believed I was good. He may have been the first person to tell me I wasn't a great singer, but he definitely wasn't the last. I knew my dad, though. I knew he loved me and wanted the best for me, and so though I was upset that the life I had envisioned for myself wasn't going to pan out, I quickly took his advice and kept writing. If anyone wanted me to be a success, he was the one. He was my dad. There was no use arguing it—I trusted him and trusted in the idea that I was positive he loved me, and so I just moved forward.

Even in recent years when I'd watch those auditions for *American Idol*,

I'd smile and almost giggle to myself because that could so easily have been me. If my dad hadn't been honest and refocused my gifts and creative energy, I could very possibly be singing in some bar as we speak, feeling underappreciated by an audience who clearly didn't recognize talent when they heard it. You see, I don't just do things—I get lost in what I'm doing. I'll do it until I feel that I'm great at it, and that would have been a lot of wasted effort considering the result would have remained the same.

I remember that talk with my father every time I have an idea or vision for myself that I think is going to be great, and then it doesn't pan out. Sometimes I will hear something about budgets at my job that makes me worry about my position there. Once I pitched what I still believe was an excellent children's devotional using wacky poetry to illustrate larger life lessons, and it was rejected from publication. Every time I try anything, I risk failure and rejection, and in those moments when I meet the worst possible scenario I have to smile and think about my dad telling me that I couldn't sing.

You see, sometimes we have plans and dreams for ourselves that God just knows aren't right for us. We see it, we feel it, and can't understand why He isn't answering or is telling us through His silence that the answer is no. Trust me: He loves you. If there is anyone who wants you to succeed in this world, it is God. Maybe it's simply time to reanalyze or refocus your gifts. Take it from me, the girl who realized the cold, hard truth of life at age 6, there is no sweeter reward in this world than finding exactly what it is God has for you to do and then doing it with all of your heart. It's the ever-sought-after meaning of life. It's the definition of fulfillment.

We all have gifts and natural abilities; some of us just don't polish them or we focus on the wrong thing, and so we miss it. I think the key is simply being able to let go. At some point you have to accept that if God is who He says He is, and if you are seeking His will for your life, then respect Him and let Him work. Maybe it isn't the right time, maybe it isn't the right place, or maybe it's just the wrong avenue for you entirely, but you have to trust that if you have sincerely sought His direction, He knows exactly how to get you from point A to point B. God doesn't need a backseat driver. He knows exactly where He is taking you.

This is probably the biggest struggle God and I go through. I am a control freak to the worst extreme. A long time ago I told Him that I was giving up my will so that His could take control. I meant that, and I still do; but so many times I get confused because the things we are passing don't look familiar, and I am sure that I have a shortcut or better way to get to where I think I need to be. I start rolling down the windows, and when I see pretty paths I tap Him on the shoulder, saying, "You sure You don't want to turn there? Are You sure that this is the right way? This just doesn't make any sense to me." I don't know if God ever rolls His eyes, but I think sometimes I tempt Him to.

Then, often at moments I least expect it, we make a pit stop. I get out, stretch my legs, and while looking around, realize where He has taken me: someplace beautiful. It's always so beautiful and special, and a complete one-of-a-kind opportunity. It's always more than I expected, and never what I envisioned. I realize in those moments that I simply think too small, and that God can't help thinking big.

A seatmate of mine in a seminarian class once told me, while I explained the current disappointment in my life, that God can bless us only with what we hand Him if we don't learn how to let His will precede our own. She said that if I hand God a measuring spoon to retrieve my blessings and tell Him exactly what I want and need, He just may fill it and hand it back to me. Little did I know that He had an entire cup. He would have loved to fill the cup and hand that back, but I didn't let Him. I asked for the spoon, I begged for the spoon, and I gave Him only a spoon to work with. In short, put down the spoon! Let God lead. He's actually really good at it.

Pray to God to remind you of your gift, and then ask for an outlet in which you can use it to His glory. One thing I have noticed is how tightly connected I have felt to Christ ever since I started writing in the hopes that it would bring Him glory. When I started using my gift for His glory, it changed our relationship. Writing is now my best form of worship. It's my time to sit and talk with Him, work with Him, and hopefully allow Him to speak through me. If I sit down and write for at least an hour a day, I cannot tell you how much more connected to Christ I feel throughout that day.

Your gift may or may not be writing. It may be singing, or speaking, or just being friendly. If you do one thing this month, I hope that it will be to figure out your gift, and figure out how God can use it. He used a few sorry loaves of bread and fish and fed thousands. He's all about making something incredible out of something incredibly small. He needs you on His team. This is a world desperate for Christians who recognize their spiritual gifts and are able to put them to use. You do have a gift. Polish it, and use it.

The truth is that I'm still a terrible singer. But I thank God every day for giving me a pen, with which I can make my own music.

Reflection: " 'For I know the plans I have for you,' declares the Lord, 'plans to prosper you and not to harm you, plans to give you hope and a future' " (Jeremiah 29:11).

Day 4

"Nobody can go back and start a new beginning,
but anyone can start today and make a new ending."
—Maria Robinson

When I was 19, I moved back home after spending my first year at college in Indiana on a track scholarship. I had gone from being a big fish in my small town's high school track program to being a minnow in a lake whipped around by a strong current. Suddenly it struck me that track, unlike basketball or football, had no real career pathway. There are only eight lanes at the Olympics, and the whole world is able to compete for them. It was safe to assume that none of those lanes were going to me.

Needless to say, after an emotionally brutal season, I came home and crawled back into my childhood bed and licked my wounds from the safety of familiarity. My first year had certainly not gone as expected. The girls all made it quite clear that they did not like me. Between snide remarks and hand-me-down gossip, they didn't leave me much room to wonder if it was all in my head. This, for a long time, was honestly the story of my life. It was really hard for me to find good girlfriends.

I must say that in recent years I have realized that the bulk of those issues said more about me than it did about them. I have now met and made the most beautiful friendships with females. Communication studies show that women rate their female friendships with higher levels of satisfaction than they do their male friendships. Surprisingly, men also rate their female friendships with higher levels of satisfaction than they do their male friendships. Don't believe the stigma that women are vicious and don't make good friends. If you develop a strong friendship with a female, you have just added a level of nurturing and commitment to your relationships that you may not have ever experienced prior.

I now recognize that girls haven't liked me because I have been pretty self-absorbed for the majority of my life. I don't mean to come off this way, and I'd be interested to take a poll among writers to see if others struggle with this same issue. But the truth is, I live in my head. I am constantly watching and thinking and writing in my head. There have honestly been so many nights that I can't will myself to sleep because my brain just never stops writing. Words plague me, and because of this I spend a great deal of my time talking to myself and having full-blown dialogue in my mind. Others may cite my lack of conversation initiative as snobby, but really I am simply already talking. Unfortunately, oftentimes it is to myself.

I remember calling my sister early in the semester with tears in my eyes, whispering from my bunk bed.

"These girls hate me here," I choked out to her.

"Why does that always happen to you?" she responded more callously than sympathetic. I hung up.

It didn't help that halfway through the first semester I had broken up with the high school boyfriend I had gone to school with. (Note to all young and in-love girls here who think following their boyfriend to college is an excellent idea: it's not! Things change, you change, and it's not high school anymore.)

There really wasn't much good that came out of that year for me. In high school I can remember lacing up my spikes in spring, just bubbling in anticipation of track season. In college I was actually physically afraid to go to the practices run by my three-time Olympic-qualifying coach. Not to mention there was this treadmill accident that had left my pride equally as bruised as my knees.

About a month into the first semester I called my mother and told her I wanted to drop out. "College isn't for me," I told her. I was not doing that well on exams I had spent hours studying for. The transition from high school to college just didn't go as smoothly as I had hoped. My mom told me that school wasn't for everyone, and that if I felt the same way by the end of the semester, we could talk about coming home and attending a community college and just doing an associate degree. Her response gave me some relief. I felt that while I might be stuck for the moment, it hopefully wouldn't last the entire year.

I honestly wasn't that great of a student in high school. I just barely finished my senior year with a 3.0 GPA. I never studied and never did homework. I just kind of flew by the seat of my pants. Suddenly I was thrust into an environment in which you actually had to do something in order to be successful, and so I tried, but it just didn't seem to be connecting. I didn't understand the skimming process. I couldn't understand why professors would assign entire chapters to read before the next class period. I would go to my room and try actually reading an entire chapter from each of my textbooks. It was exhausting. By the time I was ready to take my exams, I had studied a little of everything instead of honing in on the specific points. Ever heard the expression *jack of all trades, master of none?* That was my initial approach to college.

If you experienced or are experiencing something similar, let me give you some light at the end of the tunnel. Eventually things did connect for me. It was hard, but I transitioned. I finished my B.A. degree, M.A. degree, and now am working on a Ph.D. and teaching communications at a community college. When I think about calling my mother that day trying to drop out, I have to smile. Don't throw in the towel if something that is good for you isn't coming naturally. One of the best lessons in life is learning how to appreciate hard work. Working hard builds character. Pushing yourself is what creates growth. I wonder what I would be doing with myself right now had I dropped out of school halfway through the first semester of my first year? I would have sold myself short. No, school isn't for everyone, but you can't say it's not for you just because you don't know how to do hard work. Hard work isn't going anywhere.

Besides not particularly loving academics at first, not having many girlfriends, and breaking up with my high school boyfriend, I plain and simple chose the wrong school. I didn't think being a Seventh-day Adventist at a nondenominational college would be a problem, but it was harder than I anticipated. The second other students found out I went to church on Sabbath it seemed that they felt that I was telling them they were doing something wrong. I honestly didn't even want to address the issue, but they would ask, "Why do you go to church on Saturdays?" If I said "Because the Bible says to," it kind of created some animosity. I had a Bible teacher there who, through reading a paper, figured out I was Adventist.

"I keep the Sabbath too," he told me. He was a pastor at a mega church. "I work on Sunday, but I rest on Sabbath." I wasn't sure if I agreed with his philosophy, but it was nice to finally hear a kind word in regard to my religion, considering the backlash I had received. I have very few fond memories of that season of my life, but the impact it has left on me almost made it all worth it.

Coming home was breathtaking. It was a sense of happiness and peace I'm not sure I've ever felt before. They understood me there. My mother thought I was something really special, and my daddy always made sure everyone knew I was his baby girl.

"Those girls are just jealous!" my mom would say, brushing the hair from my face. *Finally a little compassion,* I thought to myself, glaring at my sister.

Far too often in life we rush to grow up. We have big plans for ourselves, and this tiny town just isn't big enough for them. We rush out of our childhood, not realizing how desperately we will miss it once it's gone. Every now and then it's good to stop and remember who we were before this big, bad world chewed us up and spit us out. Sometimes it takes going back to the beginning to reassess our current state.

As a child, when other kids were mean I prayed to Jesus to make them like me, and I knew He heard me. In college I never even thought to ask. Growing up, I believed that Jesus was actually my friend. For some reason, as an adult, it took going back home for me to remember that.

Jesus told the disciples in Matthew 18:3, "Truly I tell you, unless you change and become like little children, you will never enter the kingdom of heaven."

You see, when children need help, they know just who to call to make things all better. They know they are small, and so they look to someone big and trust that they will find peace with them. I think the biggest mistake we can make when it comes to God is marginalizing Him. You have to recognize that the most important part of a relationship with God is taking note of just how big He really is. He's huge. He's massive. He is everything you're not, and so we cannot live life the way we were meant to without seeking His help and guidance every moment of every day. We have to submit to being His child, which means we have to submit to His authority before we can attempt to do anything on our own. As a person, as a nation, and as a world, we desperately need His help.

You see, in my case home hadn't changed, girls hadn't really changed, and God hadn't changed. I had changed, and the second I got off my high horse long enough to recognize just how good it felt to ask for love and receive it, no questions asked, I let that love change me.

Reflection: "For I am convinced that neither death nor life, neither angels nor demons, neither the present nor the future, nor any powers, neither height nor depth, nor anything else in all creation, will be able to separate us from the love of God that is in Christ Jesus our Lord" (Romans 8:38, 39).

Day 5

met my husband when I was 10 years old. He was the cutest boy in my sixth-grade class. I loved him instantly. He, in turn, loved Katie, an adorable blond who was also in my class, but unfortunately was not me, nor did she look anything like me. I feel as though this is not the first time I sat down to write about a love interest in my childhood and was forced to reflect on how that love interest of mine was more fond of Katie. Some girls don't even have to work at it. Even at the age of 10, when the rest of us are trying to feel pretty amid our buckteeth and knobby knees, they're born blonde and flawless.

My husband was new to the school. There were only 30 some students in the whole class, so a new kid stuck out like a sore thumb. He was shorter than I was and had a bowl haircut, but made up for all of this with his amazing pair of baby-blue eyes. They were marvelous, and I just couldn't wait for the day that they would actually notice me.

I'm not making any of this up either. I know sometimes time has a funny way of creeping into our memories and smoothing out the rough edges of the past. My past is almost always documented, as even at the age of 10 I loved writing. My diary is filled to the brim with entries about Seth Day, the cutest boy in my sixth-grade class. At our wedding my father, who married us, read an excerpt from the first page of that diary, which stated clearly that I loved Seth Day and wanted to marry him.

I believe my exact words were "I love Seth Day. He doesn't like me, though. But I'll get him one day." These words being read at our wedding were really poetic justice.

Finally, one day I noticed Seth laughing at my jokes. I may not have had blond hair or blue eyes, but I did learn how to get someone to notice me. Most of the time it also landed me in after-school detentions, but at the time it was worth it. He started writing me notes, and we'd pass them all during classes.

Puppy love had finally struck his heart too, and it was my first boy-girl thing. He'd call me after school and tell me to meet him at the park. I'd pedal my bike as fast as I could, and meet him on the swing set. We'd hold hands, tell jokes, and giggle all the way till supper. I didn't really have a clue what love was, but I thought it had to be something close to the way my heart felt sitting with the cutest boy in my sixth-grade class on a pair of magical swings.

At some point the next year Seth's family moved away. He called me once or twice, but it didn't take long for him to forget all about our notes and time spent at the park. I can remember at the end of my senior year in high school, my best girlfriend made me a Facebook account. I typed "Seth Day" into the search menu in hopes that we could reconnect; I never found him, though. My second year in college I transferred to Andrews University. My mom called me right before the semester started and told me that Seth Day had just left her office. She was the associate director of Student Financial Services and saw almost every student that set foot on campus. At that point I did what any logical young woman would do in hopes of reconnecting with her childhood sweetheart. I wrote him a letter, put my phone number on it, and handed it to my mom to give to him.

He never called, and within a week I found out why. I saw him walking on campus one day with what turned out to be his long-term high school and college girlfriend, who just so happened to also be blond. Naturally I was frozen, as I suddenly felt as if I were back in sixth grade sitting invisible next to Katie. In an attempt to save what was left of my dignity, I did what I figured any girl would do in this situation. I screamed his name across campus and waved. (I told you I knew how to get someone to notice me.) I hoped that then he would think my letter was simply a letter with friendly intentions. Surely no sane woman would scream the name of someone she wanted to be romantically involved with all the way across campus, and right in front of his long-term girlfriend? Within weeks I started dating someone else, a relationship that became very serious. Two years later we were engaged, and though I had spoken with Seth many times on campus just sharing small talk, he was no longer on my mind.

The relationship I was in at that time became extremely volatile. It's crazy, because anyone who knows me would never suspect that I would allow myself to be tangled up in an abusive relationship. I had lost myself, though. He and the roller coaster of emotions we went on together consumed me. We broke up and made up daily. We screamed in each other's faces, swore, and embarrassed each other. I literally lost myself in him, and lost sight of my relationship with God as well. I was still drinking at that time in my life, and anyone who has an up-and-down relationship knows how toxic it can be, not to mention adding to that chaos the toxicities of alcohol.

Things started to get physically violent. That was really the only place left they could go. Our relationship wasn't healthy, and what I thought love was wasn't healthy either. One night, two months before my wedding, I prayed that God would intercede on my behalf. My dad had said something along the lines of "Are you sure he is the person you should be marrying?"

My parents had no clue about the level of dysfunction our relationship was in. That is another part of why toxic relationships are able to stay in motion: secrecy. You don't want to tell anyone what's actually going on because you don't think they will understand. The problem is that the second you actually hear yourself playing these incidents out loud, you realize just how perverse things have become. Perhaps this is also why therapy works. Sometimes the most sobering voice you can hear is your own. When my father expressed discomfort with my relationship, I couldn't ignore it. I had to pray.

Prayer is a scary thing for me. A long time ago I recognized that prayer was real. In the past I'd heard myself pray, and then seen God act. Prayer is powerful, and I recognized that I shouldn't say things I didn't mean or ask questions I didn't really want the answers to. This is why I hadn't prayed for God to take the matter out of my hands as of yet; I wasn't ready to let go.

"If this isn't right, and we shouldn't get married, I need You to end it for me." That one line was all I said. I literally had barely gotten "Amen" out of my mouth before my fiancé called to break up with me, because he was mad about the song I wanted to be played at the wedding. (I'm not kidding you. That is why we broke up.) This wasn't surprising to me, because we broke up all the time; but we hadn't even been fighting that day, and I had just finished my prayer. I took it hard because I knew that God was answering me. I knew that in five minutes when my fiancé would call to apologize, I couldn't accept it.

I have more than one application I would like you to take away from today's reading, one of them being that prayer works. This is precisely the reason I love reading Ellen White and sifting through her visions of Christ and angels. It reminds me of the battle that is actually going on, though I am physically blind to it.

I read a passage the other day in *Early Writings* in which Ellen refers to a vision she had of the plan for redemption. When the angels found out what Christ was going to do, they begged to take His place. They'd rather they be crucified than their Lord. Christ explained that it had to be Him, but that He did have a job for them to do in this fallen world. They were to protect us. (See pages 125-127.) When I read that, I smiled and closed the book and prayed. I realized that often when I quickly regurgitate prayers full of words I think sound good or should be said, I am forgetting that this thing is real. When I ask God to send angels to protect my daughter and husband while we are separated, I forget that there really are angels, and that this is their task. Prayer has to be real, genuine, and authentic, because God is real, genuine, and authentic. Prayer has power because God has power, and you can't just say it; you have to believe it.

What was strange this particular night was that my fiancé did not call back that evening to apologize. This had never happened before. He always cursed me out, hung up, then called 30 seconds later to go on to explain that he loved me so much and that that was why he had gotten so angry. This of course always made complete sense to me. On this night, however, 30 seconds went by, and then 30 minutes, and I still hadn't heard from him. I didn't sleep at all that night. I stayed up praying, begging God to have mercy on me, and crying my eyes out because I knew my life had to change. Finally at 2:00 in the morning my phone rang. I figured it was my fiancé, so I answered it, ready to hear his excuses.

"Is this Heather?" the voice on the other line said. I figured it was still my fiancé, or one of his friends, being weird.

"Yes," I responded.

"This is Seth, Seth Day. From sixth grade." He sounded very unsure of himself. I was so shocked I almost dropped the phone. After providing me with sufficient reminders of our past that only he would have known, I was finally satisfied that it was in fact Seth Day. For two years he had kept the note and phone number I had slipped him via my mother. He said he had thought about calling me six months after I had written him, when he and his girlfriend had broken up, but he saw me with some guy, so he figured he should wait.

Despite the obvious shock and bewilderment that I was on the phone with a boy I hadn't really spoken to since the sixth grade, I was amazed that he had kept my note for two years. I was also amazed that he was calling me from somewhere nearly two hours away, while he was at a party with some friends, on the very night that I had broken up with my fiancé. He had no idea what he had just walked into. I immediately started crying and telling him everything that had been going on in my twisted relationship. He was living in Battle Creek, an hour and a half from my home, but said he would come down tomorrow if I wanted someone to talk to. We didn't talk too long on the phone that night, maybe 10 minutes, but it was long enough to make a plan for the following day.

The next day my fiancé still had not called to apologize. In fact, I went to church and learned from my brother-in-law that he was at the bar the night before, telling everyone the wedding was off. I left church in a blur of tears and confusion, and dialed Seth. I asked him if he was still coming down that day. He said he would if I still wanted him to. I told him that I wasn't going to be great company, but that I did really need him to come and just listen to me vent, and so he did.

I should explain here that the only friends I had at this time were my friends with my ex-fiancé or friends that were supposed to be in my wedding. Everything was so fresh that I wasn't ready to talk to any of them about what had happened. When my mom finally came home, I cried and explained everything to her. I expected her to advise that I shouldn't go hang out with Seth, but she didn't. In fact, she encouraged me to go. She wanted me to breathe. She also said the timing was very ironic, and that if this boy was willing to be a friend to me right now, I should let him. Retrospectively, I realize that my mother had been praying that I would get away from my fiancé, and so she welcomed anyone who may have provided a distraction. At some point, without letting me know it, my parents had decided that they did not want me to marry that person. My dad has since told me that even though he wanted me to figure it out for myself, he was prepared to step in if I left him no choice.

About the time we said we would meet up, I saw my phone ringing with the name Seth Day on the caller ID. I didn't answer it. I was nervous because, though it felt as though I knew this person, I really didn't. He left a voice mail that said something like "Please don't tell me that I drove all the way here and now you are trying to avoid me." Honestly, if he hadn't left that message, I may not have called him back.

When we met up, my initial reaction was "Wow, this boy is gorgeous." I was obviously still very emotional and connected to my fiancé, who wasn't really my fiancé anymore, so though I took note of his physical beauty, it didn't change much of how I was feeling. When he got in my car, I immediately noticed that the boy who seemed confident and talkative on the phone was barely looking me in the eyes now. I now teach communications, and I can tell you that eye contact is the cardinal rule.

"Why aren't you looking me in the eyes when you talk to me?" I asked him frankly.

"I'm shy. Sorry. I'll work on it," he replied. His eyes were still the most enchanting form of blue, and as I watched his cheeks grow a bit red now from embarrassment, I took note again of how attractive he was.

We went to the beach and sat there for hours. The shy boy that had first entered my car started opening up to me, perhaps because I was allowing myself to be so vulnerable that it was hard for him not to. We sat by the water laughing about sixth grade and catching up on all that had happened since. My heart was too broken at that moment to think of him as anything more than a breath of fresh air from the stifled life I was living. At some point while we were at the beach, my fiancé called and left countless messages, crying and begging for my forgiveness.

I spent the rest of my summer ignoring the thousands of phone calls from my ex-fiancé, my confused bridesmaids, and my concerned friends. I literally didn't talk to anyone that whole summer, besides one girlfriend I had become very close to in the midst of my heartbreak. Well, one close girlfriend and one boy named Seth Day.

He came down to see me every weekend. He told me I was beautiful, and one day reached for my hand. Immediately my mind went right back to sixth grade and that park. At 10 my religious understanding was premature at best, but I was certain that if there was a heaven, it would have a swing set. At 22 I was certain that God was real and would intercede for me in a second if I asked Him to. I was certain, because I had seen Him do it before. Honestly, even now when my students ask how I know that there is a God, I smile and I think, *Seth Day*. I know that everyone may not understand, but that summer was a very dark place for me. I was broken, alone, and abused. I didn't know who I was anymore, and at 2:00 in the morning when I begged for mercy, God cared enough to send me the cutest boy in my sixth-grade class.

When Seth and I got married on March 6, 2011, it was the best day of my entire life. He literally saved me, and I think of him as not only my husband but also my angel. We wrote our own vows, and in front of our dearest friends and family, he swore that he would act as my earthly protector as long as God allowed. He is so much more than that. He is the kindest, sweetest man I have ever met. He is just literally that guy every dad hopes will one day take care of his baby girl. He's also much taller than I am now, with a different haircut, but still has that pair of perfect blue eyes.

The breaking up of my engagement was, at that time, the lowest moment I had seen in my life. I was humiliated, ashamed, and, to be honest, I didn't even really recognize myself anymore. I was scared to meet daylight, and in those dark hours I cried out sincerely to a God who had never really left me, but that through my own selfishness I could no longer see. My cries for direction that night changed my life. Not only because out of them I met my future husband, but because through them I watched God completely intercede for me.

When I was in high school, I wrote my first novel. It's still sitting dusty on my shelf of work I am meaning to get published. It was about an

African-American little girl growing up struggling with racism and her own race identity. One of my favorite parts of the whole book is Sam, my lead character, asking her mother what color God is. I'll end this story with an excerpt from that book, *When Rose Petals Sing.*

"It was in my first-grade year that I truly became aware of color. Macy at the supermarket was no longer just Macy; she was 'Macy the white lady.' And George at the parking garage was no longer George; he was 'George, dark like me.'

"My mother, however, always discouraged this kind of thinking. 'People are people, Samantha,' she'd always say when I referred to the 'white lady' or 'George, dark like me.' If you have a problem with their skin, take it up with God. After all, He's the one who made them, and God doesn't make dark, brown, or white. God just makes people.

"But my eyes had been torn. I didn't see people anymore; I saw skin. I saw ebony and ivory. I saw curly hair and straight hair, big lips and no lips, pitch black and brown. I saw red and yellow, pretty and ugly, pink lace and hand-me-down plaid. I saw everything I thought people were without ever seeing the person.

"It was after one of mother's racial equality speeches in third grade that I finally had the courage to ask her, 'What color is God then?'

"This was a question that had always plagued me. I didn't know if God would pity me too if He was brown like Rosy. And I didn't know if God would understand my tears if He was 'God, the white man.'

" 'God,' my mother began, 'is bright yellow when the sun rises.' She knelt down and whispered in my ear. 'And when we go to bed, He's gray like the moon. He's blue when the wind blows, and one day when you're in love, He'll be as red as roses and as bright as your smile.' She kissed my cheek and squeezed my body so tight it became hard to breathe.

" 'And what color is He when I'm crying?' I asked. A few tears ran down my cheeks and onto my mother's flawless curls.

" 'Oh baby, when you're crying,' she said, searching my eyes now, 'He's clear, so that you can't see Him holding you.' Before I could say another word, she swooped me into her arms and just held me until I forgot all about what made me cry."

I wrote that in high school, and even now at 24, it makes me smile. I guess that's the beauty of brokenness; it's in those moments that God is clear, so clear, that we can almost *see* Him holding us.

Reflection: "The Lord is close to the brokenhearted and saves those who are crushed in spirit" (Psalm 34:18).

Day 6

"All human wisdom is summed up in two words—wait and hope."
—Alexandre Dumas Père

ately some things in my life haven't been going quite as planned. I've all but given up on having much of any idea about how I see my life in the future. It seems that every time I get an idea in my head of how I want something to go, God throws something completely different at me that I wasn't expecting. His plan is always far better than the one I had for myself, but I can't help wondering why I bother obsessing over plans that never seem to take shape anyway. I think it may be better if I just start planning my life a week at a time. As long as I get to work and school on time, I should be all right. I may have to throw the towel in on any planning that goes beyond the weekend.

For example, I planned to marry my husband. I sat with my mother, cried with my father, and planned a wedding. In the sixth grade I had even prayed and planned that I would hopefully grow up to be Mrs. Seth Day. We planned the dress, the place, the cake, and the guests. What we didn't plan for was that once all the guests were gone and the wedding was over and the honeymoon started, we would get pregnant.

I was excited and nervous to tell my newly married husband that he was going to be a dad. I was happy, but at the same time, I have to explain to you that I am a planner. I plan everything. Since I was a little kid, I knew exactly what I should be doing with my life and had dates and times that I thought I should have accomplished various things. One of those things was graduate school. When Seth and I got married, I had only one month left till I would finish my master's program in communications. I had graduated with my B.A. in three and a half years, and was right on schedule to getting my doctorate before I was 30, which I had also always planned to do. None of my plans, however, included conceiving a baby while I was still on my honeymoon, and I was pretty sure Seth's didn't either.

The plan was that I would finish my doctorate, get a full-time teaching job at a university, and then Seth would be able to finish his theology degree. Our daughter completely shattered all my plans. Don't get me wrong; seeing that pregnancy test read positive was one of the most humbling and gratifying moments of my entire life. It's like in one moment a sense of responsibility and love grips your heart in a choke hold. I immediately fell to the ground and begged God to teach me how He would have me raise this child. Also in my mind, however, went all my plans as they went flashing through my brain.

At first I don't think I really thought anything had to change, but months later, when a precious little girl was kicking in my belly, getting a full-time job seemed less and less likely. I never envisioned myself as the type of woman who would want to put much of anything before her career. I had also never been pregnant before. Seeing two pink lines caused me to reprioritize my entire life, almost involuntarily. Seth told me almost immediately that he would put off his own educational dreams for me to work less and be home with the baby more. Before I had gotten pregnant, I made much more money than my husband. Since getting pregnant, however, I can't go to Taco Bell without asking him to spot me.

Pieces of me have been dying a little bit each day. I spent years creating the woman who worked hard and played later. I spent years developing the stamina to do 23 credit hours a semester and finish with all A's. It took a lot of hard work to do my M.A. program from 7:00 a.m. to 12:00 p.m. and then go to work at 2:00 p.m. and not get home till almost midnight. I did this every single day because I wanted to be successful, and, for me, success came with a degree that read Ph.D. If I didn't meet my time lines, did that mean I wasn't successful? It's like I am sitting with a giant puzzle trying to jam all these pieces of my "planned" life into place, but none of them fit. All I can think about is raising my daughter and making sure I provide for her an excellent example of what not only a woman looks like but what a relationship with God looks like.

I sincerely believe that Christ is returning shortly. I also believe that many of us think we are prepared, and aren't. I think Satan is gunning for the fact that we are comfortable with our Christianity. We compare our church to the Laodiceans in Revelation. When I read that verse that says Christ would rather you be cold or hot than lukewarm, I didn't really understand the lukewarm terminology until this past week.

Revelations 3:14-16 says, "To the angel of the church in Laodicea write:

These are the words of the Amen, the faithful and true witness, the ruler of God's creation. I know your deeds, that you are neither cold nor hot. I wish you were either one or the other! So, because you are lukewarm—neither hot nor cold—I am about to spit you out of my mouth."

You see, I used to think that being lukewarm was wrong because you were wishy-washy. I thought that the problem was that you hadn't really made up your mind, and I honestly didn't understand why God would rather you be cold than lukewarm. Recently, though, I have been spending a great deal of time in prayer and Scripture. (Another perk of not working full-time.) This past week I realized why God would rather you be cold than lukewarm. Because when we are lukewarm, we are comfortable in our warmness. We feel that we've got a lot of things right, and so we think we are prepared. You see, it's harder for God to reach a comfortable Christian than a cold Christian, because at least a cold Christian knows they are cold. They sense the emptiness, and so God has things He can do to make us realize how radically wrong we are.

How does He shake up someone who has no idea they even have a problem? Indeed, I believe the church of Laodicea is much like the church of today. We are comfortable. We think we've got a lot of right answers, and so we think we are prepared to meet the days of trouble. Let me tell you this: if you can look at yourself and recognize that you do not reflect Christ fully, then you are not ready, and you should not be comfortable. God wants you to live your life like wet clay for His molding. If Satan has his way, though, your comfort will leave you stiff.

When Christ descends from those clouds and every eye sees Him, I want to be able to stand and meet Him. I want to be able to stand in His radiance. If I do not prepare my heart and mind to reflect the image of Christ fully, there is simply no way I will be able to meet that kind of holiness and continue standing. I want to finish this race on my feet, but suddenly more important than that, I want to see my daughter on hers. Lately I feel as if a thousand weights are sitting on my chest. The more convicted I become that Christ is telling me to prepare myself for the end of days, the more I feel compelled to make sure that every loved one I hold dear is prepared as well, my daughter being my first priority. I think we underestimate the responsibility that comes with not just being a parent but a Christian. You will be held accountable for all that you did not say. You must find your voice because lives depend on it.

Yesterday morning I was sitting at our kitchen table reading my morning devotional. I am currently almost finished with Ellen White's *Patriarchs and Prophets*. (An excellent read, by the way.) I was reading about David and how after Samuel anointed him to be king over all of Israel, he went right back to tending sheep and playing music alone in the woods and did this for years. (See chapter 62.) That thought transfixed me. Here's this normal kid, the youngest of all his brothers, finding out that his destiny is to be king over his entire land, but in the meantime all he can do is watch out for his sheep. White says in the book that David was content to await the greater purpose of his life, and that he used that time in the fields building his relationship with Christ (p. 641).

Right after I read that I knelt on my knees and prayed. Now I try to address God only when on my knees if I can. I think it helps remind me that He is the Creator of the universe, and that the only place I really have to communicate anything to Him is from on my knees. I get on my knees and press my nose to the floor, and that's how I pray now. It's really done something powerful to our relationship. It reminds me, during the moments when I get too comfortable and tend to marginalize Christ, that I have to be ever cognizant that this is the King of kings with whom I speak. When my face is pressed to the floor, it allows me to take prayer seriously because God is real and He can hear me; and through prayer I invite Him to commune with me. If I am going to talk to my Creator, I am certainly going to do it with reverence. I can't really fully explain how much this simple act has changed my worship, except to ask you to try it for yourself. I spoke with God that morning and thanked Him for the reading of David at that moment in my life that I was feeling discontent.

Perhaps you're feeling in your life the way I am feeling in mine—a bit misplaced. I feel that I have had to slow down a bit to reprioritize and refocus my energies. I want to be an excellent mother. I want that to be my main focus right now, and I had been feeling sort of bad about it. I realized yesterday, though, that much like David, sometimes it's good to do nothing but catch your breath. Slow down and focus on nothing more than your current set of circumstances, and building your relationship with God.

My "pause" button is a child, but yours may be completely different. Maybe a financial hardship or an illness or some type of unexpected family issue has come up, and suddenly you have to put plans on hold for a moment. I learned through David's story that that is OK. Big things are still awaiting you, and a pause just may be part of the preparation to get you there. If the future king of Israel could enjoy tending sheep and bonding with God, I am sure you and I can make this time a positive one as well. Perhaps had David not had those years to reflect, he would not have been Israel's most revered king. Perhaps by slowing down, you are actually taking a giant leap forward.

I have come to realize that I may never meet and accomplish all my plans and objectives. I may have to sit and watch as every one of my plans crumble in my hands like grains of sand. In the end, does it really matter if my life doesn't go according to my plans? In fact, now I hope it doesn't. You see, the closer to God I get, the more secure I feel in acknowledging my own weakness. My plans mean nothing; it is His plans for my life that I better move heaven and earth to see accomplished.

Reflection: "But those who hope in the Lord will renew their strength. They will soar on wings like eagles; they will run and not grow weary, they will walk and not be faint" (Isaiah 40:31).

Day 7

"There are always three speeches, for every one you actually gave.
The one you practiced, the one you gave,
and the one you wish you gave."

—Dale Carnegie

love teaching communications courses. On the first day of class, when I look across the sea of students that will be joining me in a journey that semester, I always tell them the same thing: Communications, unlike many other college courses you are going to take, has the ability to change your life. I do not say that to slander history, math, or any of the sciences. I say it because communications is the essence of the human experience. With good communication skills a person can get the job they want, the girl they want, the guy they want, sometimes even the life they want. Studies show that communication is a skill that the average person is not very good at, and yet most people don't even realize it.

The textbook I teach from says that the definition of a competent communicator is being able to change your message to fit your audience. How often in life do you hear people say, "Well, if they don't get what I am saying, that's their problem"? I tell my students that that arrogant thinking is exactly why most Americans are no longer competent in communicating. It is, in fact, your problem. If you don't learn how to craft your message so that your audience can understand it, you will never get anything done. You can see this play out in the Bible as well. How many times does God not just say something but finds a way for it to connect to the person He is saying it to so that they completely understand?

For example, let's look at the prophet Jeremiah. The Bible tells this story in Jeremiah 13:1-11: "This is what the Lord said to me: 'Go and buy a linen belt and put it around your waist, but do not let it touch water.' So I bought a belt, as the Lord directed, and put it around my waist. Then the word of the Lord came to me a second time: 'Take the belt you bought and are wearing around your waist, and go now to Perath and hide it there in a crevice in the rocks.' So I went and hid it at Perath, as the Lord told me.

Many days later the Lord said to me, 'Go now to Perath and get the belt I told you to hide there.' So I went to Perath and dug up the belt and took it from the place where I had hidden it, but now it was ruined and completely useless."

And then here we see God, in His communication genius, make His application. Verse 8 continues: "Then the word of the Lord came to me: 'This is what the Lord says: "In the same way I will ruin the pride of Judah and the great pride of Jerusalem. These wicked people, who refuse to listen to my words, who follow the stubbornness of their hearts and go after other gods to serve and worship them, will be like this belt—completely useless! For as a belt is bound around the waist, so I bound all the people of Israel and all the people of Judah to me," declares the Lord, "to be my people for my renown and praise and honor. But they have not listened." ' "

I love biblical examples like this of God's complete genius. Perhaps it is the communication academic in me, but I have highlighted all the verses like this one in my Bible, because it is awesome for me to see how God doesn't just say something; He provides a way to make sure we understand what He is saying. He adjusts His message to fit His audience. Jeremiah fully understands now the message he is to give to the people. God cannot just say, "Well, if they don't get what I am saying, that is their problem," because then what is the point in saying anything at all?

The point of communication is for person A to send message B to person C. Communication does not take place if B, the message, is not understood. It's not good enough if they think they understand or get an idea of the main point. If the exact message that person A sent does not get to person C crystal clear, then it is simply not communication. Once you understand that, you are on your way to communicating messages competently.

What is really fun is teaching a public speaking course. As the instructor of that course, you can be certain that 99 percent of your student population does not want to be in your classroom. In fact, many studies show that glossophobia, the fear of public speaking, ranks with many people right up there with the fear of death. In short, many of my students would rather die than be in my classroom. Every time I talk, I am prepared for everyone's eyes to divert to anyplace in the room besides connecting with mine. They think that maybe if they aren't looking at me directly, then they will somehow be able to magically disappear.

At a doctoral seminar my instructor told me about a method that he used to ease the anxiety of public speaking a bit. I have since adopted that method, and have had every student do it on the first day of class. I ask everyone to take out a piece of paper and, using the hand that they do not typically write with, write their name across the center of the paper and then show it to the person next to them. Of course everyone's is terrible. My handwriting is childlike even with my correct hand, so with my other one it is almost unintelligible.

After this experiment I inform them that public speaking, much like writing with your other hand, is a learned behavior. If every night that semester those students went home and wrote their names with their opposite hand for just 10 minutes an evening, by the end of the semester they would be ambidextrous. In the same light, if every night they go home and hopefully spend a little more than 10 minutes a day writing and preparing for their speeches, by the end of the semester they will leave my classroom being able to speak publicly almost anywhere. That is the beauty of learned behaviors: If you practice, you can master them.

It is my belief that love is also a learned behavior. Just like public speaking, some of us may be born a little bit more comfortable with it than others; however, with practice, any of us can do it. My parents tell me that when I was a child, I was quite the bully. They actually sat with me for 10 or so minutes every evening just to hold me and repeat, "Love, Heather, you need to love." If I saw a kid with a bottle I wanted, I knocked that kid over and took it. If someone had a toy that I liked, I was going to enjoy that toy too by any means necessary, which usually was force. I was not born loving.

Sometimes if I feel the need to, I'll tell my students that in the eighth grade I was the first student ever expelled from my Seventh-day Adventist elementary school. Without fail, every time I say it they spend at least five minutes asking me if I'm pulling their leg.

"But you're so nice!" I always hear. I think the difference between me and a lot of people is that even when I was little, whatever I was thinking, I usually said. To this day, it is extremely hard for me to fake or pretend. That's why even when I get gifts for my birthday, I dread opening them in front of whoever got them for me. I am so nervous that if I don't actually like a gift, I won't be able to fake it and make you believe I do. I have always been this way, so even when I was a child, if I didn't feel like being nice, then, unlike a lot of other little girls, I simply wasn't. If I didn't actually like you, you probably knew it. To this day, it makes my heart skip beats to hear people describe me as nice, because for so long I was told I was the opposite.

When I became a Christian and truly fell in love with Jesus, I knew that I would have to smooth out the rough edges of my personality. I knew God could not use me if I did not learn to sincerely love and appreciate His other children for who they were. I feel that as I say this a lot of people are thinking, *Glad that's not my problem; I'm nice to everyone.* But are you really? I don't mean nice to people's faces and then saying what you really think behind their backs. I sincerely try to live my life thinking, *If I would not say this to that person's face, I am not going to share it with anyone else.* I want to smile at you and have you know I mean it. I want people to meet me and sense that I care about them sincerely. If you haven't yet noticed, one running theme in this book is my sense of urgency that we must start preparing to reflect Christ fully. That is the message that God has put on my heart to share, and so that is why I keep repeating it, as if I have only one tool in my toolbox.

I believe that Christ is coming, and that this generation, my generation, is going to be the church of the last days. We are Laodicea, and lukewarm Christianity is not going to cut it. God has a lot of characteristics with which we could describe Him, but the greatest of them all is love. If we do not learn to reflect that same love, we are going to be in trouble.

The Bible tells us that it is essential to master this thing of love. First John 4:16 says, "And so we know and rely on the love God has for us. God is love. Whoever lives in love lives in God, and God in them." In order for Christ to live in you, in order for you to fully reflect Him, you must love.

In order to make sure I am communicating competently, let me make sure we both have the same idea of what it means to love. John 14:21 says, "Whoever has my commands and keeps them is the one who loves me. The one who loves me will be loved by my Father, and I too will love them and show myself to them." So in order to love Christ, we must follow His teachings and keep His commandments. We can't just assume that believing in Christ means we love Him. Satan believes in Christ. You must believe in Him and follow His commandments and teachings. If you do not do this, you do not truly love Him.

Again, we see in Joshua 22:5, "But be very careful to keep the commandment and the law that Moses the servant of the Lord gave you: to love the Lord your God, to walk in obedience to him, to keep his commands, to hold fast to him and to serve him with all your heart and with all your soul." Here we recognize that loving God requires obedience to Him.

And again, we see similar language in Deuteronomy 10:12, 13: "And now, Israel, what does the Lord your God ask of you but to fear the Lord your God, to walk in obedience to him to love him, to serve the Lord your God with all your heart and with all your soul, and to observe the Lord's commands and decrees that I am giving you today for your own good?" So by proving our love for God, we follow His commandments and teachings, which, out of love, He provided for us. In order to reflect Christ fully, we must learn to love.

I overheard my nephew's mother telling my dad the other day that people can just sense Christ living in him. A huge smile crept on my face as I thought that that had to be the best compliment you could ever give someone. Imagine if people met you and sensed that Christ was living in you. I guess that can only be a powerful thought to you if you know firsthand how incredible Christ really is.

Maybe you are a naturally sincere person, and there is no hypocrisy in your veins. Or maybe you are like me, and praying for God to smooth out a few more of your personality wrinkles. At any rate, I have good news for you. Love, like public speaking, is a learned behavior. It doesn't really matter what all you're not. All that matters is everything God is. Perhaps just maybe, if we spend a little more time with Him than we have been spending, we will learn to love. And maybe someday others who meet us will, without our preaching it, sense that we've been practicing writing His name with our incorrect hand, all over our hearts.

Reflection: "But whoever is united with the Lord is one with him in spirit" (1 Corinthians 6:17).

Day 8

"It is loneliness that makes the loudest noise.
This is true of men as of dogs."
—Eric Hoffer

After class one day I had a student from a public speaking course ask me if she could do her important-person speech on Jesus. I teach at a public community college, and it just isn't every day that people want to get up and talk about God. I have heard speeches on all types of things. A recurring one for persuasive speeches is that we should legalize marijuana. Seriously, every semester, without fail, at least two students will get up and give that speech. I would like to teach at a Christian university one day, but for now I believe I am exactly where God wants me.

I enjoy that the people here are real. There is no pretending to be someone you're not, and sometimes I find it refreshing. There is something to be said about humanity in its rawest form. It almost always forces you to feel an emotion. I once heard someone say that the key to being successful is to force people to have an opinion about you, one way or the other. People being candid about their struggles and triumphs forces you to do just that—love them or hate them. I have a friend who posted a Facebook status that said "Don't hate me because I don't sin like you do."

For an example of the attitude I typically encounter: one day I had a guest speaker in my class. His name is Elroy Byam, and he is one of the best freestyle poets I have ever heard. The pen is a well-crafted and trained instrument in his hands. He is a Seventh-day Adventist, as am I, and I asked him to speak to my communications class while we were in the chapter on verbal communication. During his seminar he wanted to illustrate the point that you do not get up in front of a live audience and communicate a message that you have not first dated, fell in love with, and then married.

"Who is married in here?" he asked. Community college provides a vast array of students, and I like that about it also. I have nontraditional and traditional students all in the same classroom. At 24 years of age, I am often, in my night classes, the youngest person in the room. A few raised their hands in answer to his question. He selected a woman at random and asked her to tell the process that led up to her marrying her husband.

Because Elroy and I are from similar Christian backgrounds, we both thought we knew the answer she would provide. We both had similar views on marriage, and assumed that everyone did. These are a few of the mistakes I still tend to make when meeting people—assuming that we are all the same and think the same. I can't tell you how many times at the end of a semester I find out a student I've been working with for a while now is gay, or has been sexually abused, or is an atheist, or studying Eastern pantheistic worldviews and is very intrigued by Buddhism. This is why in secular institutions you can't use classtime to talk about your own personal religious choices, because there are so many in attendance with completely different perspectives.

There are moments I appreciate this, because instead of always coming to bat with my theistic ideology, I can first form relationships. As Allan Walshe, my seminary professor, told us, you won't actually convert people from a pulpit. It has to be through relationships. I also don't keep my beliefs to myself. At some point during our semester together my students always ask me about my worldview. Probably because I often pray that someone will. And when they do ask, I tell them, and because a relationship is there, they listen.

When Elroy asked the woman about the process that led to her marriage, he expected her to state linearly the process of dating, falling in love, and then the decision to commit and get married. He was going to use that to explain that with the same token we should handle our verbal messages. If we have to give a speech, first we have to write it, and in a sense that phase is when we "date" the material. Next, we have to practice it, and that is when we are "falling in love." Last, we should have practiced that speech so much that we know it like the back of our hand before we ever deliver it. That is the commitment, or the "marrying," of your verbal messages. His point is that we should never deliver a message without knowing it and being passionate about that message.

"So tell me," he asked, "what was the process that led you to marrying your husband?"

"Tequila," she answered.

"Tequila?" he questioned.

"Well," she continued, "I got really drunk off tequila one night and ended up having a one-night stand. I found out I was pregnant, and we got married. So, tequila was the process that led to my marriage."

So you see, these are the types of statements I am used to hearing. Quite often I get responses that knock you off your feet, and as the head of the classroom, this leaves your brain scrambling with how to get things back in the direction you need them to go.

I suppose I should not just put these categories in my secular box. I have had similar experiences with Christians. In the Bible study I attend, my friend Tyler had prepared a study on varying issues our generation has with the Bible. He started the study by stating, "I just want to go around the room and ask how many of us believe the earth was created in six literal days."

Honestly, in my mind I thought, *What a waste of time.* He turned to the very first person and asked if they believed the earth was created in six literal days, and their response was "Not necessarily."

I was floored. He continued around the room, and every single person said that while they were sure God could create the world in six days, they didn't think He did. Here we were, all professed Christians, all needing and wanting Bible study, and yet we were undecided on the very first line of Scripture. Quite honestly, I was shaking by the time he got to me. I tend to get really excited whenever someone indulges me with conversation about God in general, and I was experiencing an overwhelming mix of emotions that these friends I had made didn't believe that God created the world in six literal days. A couple weeks before, my husband had already gone through with his study establishing the validity of the Bible, and no one said a peep.

"I'm positive that the earth was created in six literal days," I said, trying to seem calm.

"How can you be positive? Don't you think that's a bit arrogant?" someone responded.

"No. When it comes to certain basics of my theology, I am absolutely certain of what I believe. I have to be," I said.

One thing I have also noticed in our Bible studies is that this generation seems uncomfortable addressing truth. It's a mark of the postmodern generations. We believe all truth is relative and that there is no such thing as absolute truth. I see this take shape when people have a hard time just saying that they believe in God and His Word as the ultimate truth, even if they are Christians. It's hard for them to be 100 percent certain of anything, because truth is relative.

I also had to ask them why they felt the need to say that it wasn't six literal days. I knew that the answer would be science. You can't bend Scripture to fit science, though, and if you feel the need to do so, you are going to finish disappointed. I went on to explain that I believed the earth was created in six literal days, because that is why my church rests on the seventh day of the week; in homage to what God did at Creation. I also referenced the Ten Commandments, the only portion of the Bible that Christ wrote Himself.

Exodus 20:8-11 says, "Remember the Sabbath day by keeping it holy. Six days you shall labor and do all your work, but the seventh day is a sabbath to the Lord your God. On it you shall not do any work, neither you, nor your son or daughter, nor your male or female servant, nor your animals, nor any foreigner residing in your towns. For in six days the Lord made the heavens and the earth, the sea, and all that is in them, but he rested on the seventh day. Therefore the Lord blessed the Sabbath day and made it holy."

Now, if it says again that in six days the Lord made the heavens and the earth in the Ten Commandments, how can you still think that this may be symbolism? The Bible seems pretty clear, in my opinion, on the issue. The account in Genesis 1:1-31 even says, "And there was evening, and there was morning," to mark the end of the days.

Genesis 1:1-5 says, "In the beginning God created the heavens and the earth. Now the earth was formless and empty, darkness was over the surface of the deep, and the Spirit of God was hovering over the waters. And God said, 'Let there be light,' and there was light. God saw that the light was good, and he separated the light from the darkness. God called the light 'day,' and the darkness he called 'night.' And there was evening, and there was morning—the first day."

To me, God couldn't have made it any clearer than this. He even created morning and evening first, so that the rest of creation can be marked by time. From morning and evening He created a period of time called a day. This was not by happenstance; God is intentional with everything He does. In my parting words on the subject to them, I said that if they couldn't take the very first words on the very first page of Scripture to simply say what they mean, I was worried about their approach to the rest of the Bible. In my opinion, this is exactly why there are so many nonbelievers, because believers can make things very confusing. I was sure I ruffled a few feathers when I was finished, but I felt it was important to be firm on the issue.

At any rate, when a student approached me asking if she could do her speech about how she had met Christ, I was bubbling with joy. She was a nontraditional student and had spent the majority of her life working in a factory that had closed when the economy went south. The next day when she gave her speech, she told the class that she had met Jesus when she was 7 years old. She spoke about how she was the youngest of her other siblings, and often felt left out. At 7 she started to spend a lot of time sitting and thinking under her parents' lilac tree. During one of those lonely afternoons at the age of 7, she said that Jesus actually physically visited her.

"I wasn't afraid when I saw Him," she said. "I knew He had simply stopped by so that I would have a friend." After a few minutes He was gone, and she ran inside to tell her mother whom she had just seen. It was the end of the 1960s, and most families owned a large picture Bible that they could read with the kids.

"What did the man look like?" her mother asked her. She went to the picture Bible, opened it up to a picture of Jesus, and said, "This was Him, Mommy."

"Well," her mother told her, "you must be a very special little girl for Jesus to come visit you." At the conclusion of her speech she spoke the words I am sure everyone was thinking.

"In my life," she said, "I haven't really felt all that special. I often wonder if Jesus visited me that day because I had something I was supposed to do with my life and never did. I'm certainly no one special, and have spent most of my life working in a factory. For a long time I could not understand why Jesus would ever choose to visit me." She lowered her head a bit, and I watched as her lips quivered.

"Recently," she continued, "I decided that there could be only one reason that Jesus would ever want to meet with me under the lilac tree that day." She stopped and looked up, meeting the gaze of the entire classroom, who were all silent, waiting to hear what she would say.

"The only thing I can think of as to why Jesus would visit me is that I was important to Him." Her quivering lips fell still and then curved into a smile, and she sat down.

Her speech shook me the rest of the day and into the days to come. In all honesty, when she first said she met Christ face to face, my very first thought was *Well, why would Christ meet you and not me? I read my Bible, probably more than you do. I pray, probably more than you do, and He hasn't met with me face to face.* In fact, I have spent many nights begging to simply hear His voice, and to this day have never heard Him speak to me verbally.

It's funny, because in our own minds, we think we have to really be someone to get God to care about us, let alone to visit us face to face. What I find comical is that in the scheme of heaven and the angels, whatever big shot you are on earth probably means nothing. We have all sinned and fallen short of the glory of God. Our biggest deal, our most talented, or educated, or rich, or beautiful, or strongest person, falls tremendously in comparison to whatever concept we think worthy to meet face to face with God.

What if we all went back to the basics? What if the only criterion we needed to believe that God loved us, or even harder, to believe that God loved other people who we, or this world, didn't see as "special enough" to meet His standards, was simple? What if the only reason we needed to love each other was equally as basic?

My heart was ripped open by that student that day because I realized how unpretentious God really is. Yes, I believe that in the 1960s there was a lonely little girl who did not feel special and spent afternoons secluded under a lilac tree. I also believe that Jesus visited her once, and not because of anything extraordinary, but simply because she was His, and because she was important to Him.

Reflection: "The King will reply, 'Truly I tell you, whatever you did for one of the least of these brothers and sisters of mine, you did for me'" (Matthew 25:40).

Day 9

I always wondered what my first love would be like. I wondered if I'd feel butterflies and hum songs and forget that the tune I was singing was his name. I wondered if love really was the closest thing to magic, and if the sun and wind would write me love letters and seal them with his kiss. I think every girl wants that. Something real, something she can hang her heart on and know is sturdy.

I wanted to be kissed. Not just any ole kiss, either; I wanted "the" kiss. The "open mouths, almost blackout mid-kiss" kiss. The "brush the strands of hair from your face" kiss, and the "hold your breath until it's over" kiss. I wanted the kiss that I'd spend the next three days solely pondering, and the kiss that I'd compare every other kiss to. I wanted the "stare into each other's eyes" kiss. The "Romeo and Juliet, thunder and lightning, entire world goes on hold" kiss. I wanted to have his lips reach my soul and plant my hand upon his heart. I wanted to be rocked to the core, and forever changed. I wanted to breathe his breath. I wanted to see what love tasted like, and I thought that a kiss like that would show me.

The first time I actually did kiss a boy, I was a sophomore in high school. I started dating my first serious boyfriend, and I stayed with him until October of my senior year. His sister is to this day my best friend in the whole world, and whom I know I wouldn't have met had I not dated him. It is that thought that often reminds me that so many things in life, though seemingly purposeless at the time, often do happen for a reason.

During my first year I had been talking to a boy we'll call Ralph. He was quarterback on his large high school's football team. I remember one time I went to one of his games, and during his warm-up he spotted me in the stands and pointed the football right at me and smiled. I felt like a movie star at that moment, and half wanted to stand up so that everyone else in the bleachers could get a good look at the girl who had just received such a romantic gesture.

I went to meet him one night at the beach's annual Fourth of July fireworks. After the display was over, a group of us kids were all just hanging out talking on the sand. My parents kept me on a pretty tight leash, so I knew it was probably time that I find my sister in this mob and go home. We stood there talking for a bit under the awnings of the food stand because it was starting to rain and I was hesitant to get my hair wet.

"You aren't afraid of a little rain, are you?" he asked me with a half smile.

"Of course not," I chimed back. "I love rain!"

The truth was that I hated rain. It always destroyed the hair I had spent hours straightening. The second that water touched it, I knew my head would be an Afro, and not the attractive kind. Thunder cracked, and I shrieked a bit at the thought of standing in front of him for even a second as my hair turned into a mop.

"Thought you said you didn't mind the rain," he chuckled.

"I lied," I said, laughing and turning my head to meet his gaze.

I thought he was going to kiss me. The moment was right, and I would have just melted right there if I was able to go home and tell my older sister, Natasha, that I had been kissed. I straightened my shoulders and batted my eyelashes the way the girls in movies did right before their lips pursed. I blinked a few times slowly and remembered watching Natasha kiss her high school sweetheart from my window the week before. I had filled the words in for their moving lips and wished deeply that I were her as he leaned forward and cupped her face. I didn't need to wish anymore, because my moment was better than hers. I was Heather and he was Ralph. And I could bet that my sister's boyfriend didn't know a thing about kissing in the rain.

He grabbed my shoulders and drew me into his chest. My heart stopped and my body stood frozen, afraid to breathe. He hugged me tight, put his arm around my shoulders, and started walking back toward his friends. No kiss. Instead, I got a pat on the shoulder. Not quite the romantic gesture I was hoping for.

It's funny, because as I think about that picture now, I can't help thinking about my husband. As a teenage girl I daydreamed about being the recipient of this incredible, life-altering kiss, and if I am honest, I didn't get that kiss till him. My best friend can attest that the first time I kissed my husband it was literally everything I had ever imagined a kiss to be, and more. I couldn't get him out of my mind. It was summer, and I was 22 years old. He had logged probably 100 hours of phone conversation with me and had driven the hour and a half to see me every weekend. He was the most affectionate man I had ever met. He was always putting his arm around me or holding my hand or putting his face very close to mine while I talked.

I was not used to this. My ex-fiancé and I were more of best friends than romantic partners. We were together because we had fun together. He made me laugh. My husband is the first guy I ever dated whom I wanted people to see me out with. He was so handsome and just made me feel that I was always the only girl in the room. It wasn't that I was so intrigued by all the funny things he said—if anything, I was mesmerized by how he didn't have to say a word. He is also the smartest guy I have ever dated. He thought about real life-provoking questions. Life and decisions mattered to him, and I felt more alive in his presence.

They say that if you take an event and match it to an emotion, that is how you create memories, because an event combined with an emotion burns an image of that event into your mind, and you will remember it forever. I thought I knew what love was before my husband, but obviously I didn't have a clue. His kiss is the only kiss I can honestly remember, and I think it's because I loved him in a way I wasn't sure existed outside of romance novels and love movies. Often he'd kiss me while I was in the middle of saying something. I have a crystal-clear memory of us buying groceries, and as I asked which type of chips he'd prefer, he interrupted my sentence to kiss me. Normally I'd be humiliated because I am not really one for public displays of affection, but it was Seth, and so I melted from his "rude" interruption. He's given me so many perfectly clear memories.

I almost settled for counterfeit love. I even almost married someone else. I am so lucky and grateful to God that I recognized His voice and did an about-face, ending the engagement I was in just before meeting Seth. Marriage seems hard enough if you've got it right and are with the man of your dreams.

This is not to say that my husband, who is definitely my soulmate, doesn't also drive me crazy sometimes. The other day I came home to find a cereal box in the refrigerator and milk in the pantry. Clearly Seth had had breakfast. I went to my room to change out of my work clothes and found an apple core under my bed. Ah, Seth had had a snack while taking a catnap on his lunch break. I love the man to death, but the sheer fact that

I am a woman and he is a man says that we are going to be worlds apart on some of our habits and thinking. I am sure I drive him crazy too. My husband is a man of very few words, and I want to talk about everything. When he has a bad day, I want him to tell me about it. He doesn't want to tell me about it. He wants to lie down, zone out, and accidentally leave an apple core under the bed. Men: Can't live with them, can't live without them, I guess.

Two weeks after my disappointing shoulder pat, it was the Venetian Festival at the beach, which brought in even more people than the Fourth of July and had even better fireworks. It was pretty much a carnival on the sand, and everybody who was anybody in high school was there. I didn't care about anyone else; I just wanted to see Ralph. Finally, after pushing my way through a throng of people, I found a few of his friends on a sidewalk, although I didn't see him.

"Are you Ralph's girlfriend?" one of them asked. My cheeks were hot. He hadn't asked me to be his girlfriend, but I figured I practically was. We had gone to the movies together, talked on the phone—I had even met his parents.

"I don't know," I smiled. "Why?"

"Oh, I was just wondering," he smiled back. "Because he's over there with another girl."

I couldn't believe it. Sure enough, as I followed his pointing finger, my eyes located Ralph with his arms around a beautiful Asian girl who was smoking a cigarette. Not only was she not me, but she made me look like a little girl in comparison. She had to be a senior. The only thought I kept my mind fixed on was *Don't cry, don't cry, don't cry.*

It was dark, and their smiling faces were almost illuminated by the carnival lights. I watched as he put his arm around her shoulders and whispered in her ear. I wondered if he would laugh with her about the rain too, or stand with her under its beads while they shared their first kiss. Certainly it would not be her first kiss. This girl had definitely been kissed before. I felt so small standing there being pummeled by the sounds of carnival music, laughing teenagers, and their illuminated faces.

"Ralph's a jerk, Heather," one of his friends said, probably nervous that I wouldn't be able to hold the water in my eyes from falling down my cheeks right in front of them.

"Yeah," I managed to choke out. I would have run home had the beach not been a 25-minute drive from my house.

"I love you, Heather," my best friend Tracy said, squeezing a tight hold on to my hand. Her skin was tan and made her blond hair look platinum. I followed her lead away from his friends, and hoped that the growing crowd would just swallow me whole so that I could avoid any humiliating encounters between me and them.

I think that night was one of the first times I realized how imperfect life was. My heart was literally shattered, but somehow I got through it. I watched from the sidelines as a beautiful girl got to live my dream with the person I thought was my guy while I stood almost 50 feet away embarrassed and alone. Sometimes there just isn't a happy ending, and those are the toughest pills to swallow. Obviously, when I was 15 I didn't think I'd make it through the night, but I did, and I am alive to tell the tale.

Sometimes things are going to be bad. You're going to be lost, and there just won't be a happy ending. There are going to be moments that you draw the shortest stick. Whether you're 15, 25, or 51, there will be days and nights that you swear you won't live through. But you will.

God doesn't promise that we can live through anything; He promises that with His help, we will find strength. People are often shocked to find out that the verse we often tell each other about God not giving us more than we can bear actually does not exist.

The verse people are referring to is 1 Corinthians 10:13, and it says, "No temptation has overtaken you except what is common to mankind. And God is faithful; he will not let you be tempted beyond what you can bear. But when you are tempted, he will also provide a way out so that you can endure it."

What God does promise is that He will provide a way out if we remain faithful, and that with His help we will make it. The good news is that God will hold you as you mourn the death of a friend, just as He held me tight when I was 15 years old and a boy broke my heart. He deals with us individually and handles our problems with precise tenderness. At some point in your life you will probably be dealt something more than you can bear, but remember, with Christ you will make it through the toughest nights. Besides, it takes hell's hot fire to make heaven-ready steel.

Reflection: "I can do everything through him who gives me strength" (Philippians 4:13).

Day 10

"At the Day of Judgment, we shall not be asked
what we have read, but what we have done."

—Thomas à Kempis

As a kid, one of my favorite stories in the Bible was the battle of Jericho. For a small child who often felt that the entire world was against her, I took great faith in the courage of Joshua. By faith, for six days the Israelites marched in silence around the great city walls. What a sight I imagined they must have been to their opponents. This is where *faith* comes into play. I don't think it takes as much faith to believe in God, because I think we have so many evidences that prove His existence. To me, faith in the Christian experience comes into play when you feel Him calling you to some place outside of your comfort zone, or asking you to do something that doesn't make much sense to you. I believe that believing in God as the Creator of the universe has a lot of empirically sound evidence, whereas following that still small voice of God to wherever He may be leading you seems to take a great deal of faith, and sometimes blind faith. Surely Joshua felt confident during this march, because the angel of the Lord had met with him personally, instructing him on what to do.

We should note that the Israelites had just finished crossing the Jordan, where by divine power the water was made dry. This is the first time since they left Egypt that we see God dry up water so that His children can walk on dry land. The people of Israel have endured a lot since leaving Egypt. Most of the people who left Egypt have all died, including Moses. Joshua and Caleb are the only ones who get to see this miracle again after wandering the desert for 40 years.

Because the Jordan has just dried up, neighboring Canaanite kings are afraid of the Israelites. They are afraid because the Jordan was their main line of defense, and it was even flood season. They were not guarding the Jordan, because they figured there was no way the Israelites could penetrate it. They had heard of a God who dried up the Red Sea so that His children could walk over it, and that same God has just acted again. The power of this God, and the love He has for His people, scares them.

Now, to all of Israel, that would probably seem like the best time to attack Jericho. The people are afraid; they are in disarray. The Bible says that their hearts were melted and they lost their courage to face the Israelites. Now, Joshua is a great warrior, and I am sure it doesn't take long for him to realize that an imminent attack on Jericho is probably the best option. There is no reason to wait; the time is now. Of course, God always has another plan.

Before they can move forward, God instructs Joshua that the people of Israel need to undergo circumcision. Why would God do this? The time is right to wage war, and God wants them to stop and undergo circumcision? Surely this will cause the Israelite men to need time to heal and rest.

We see God's reasoning for this in Joshua 5:4-8: "Now this is why he did so: All those who came out of Egypt—all the men of military age—died in the wilderness on the way after leaving Egypt. All the people that came out had been circumcised, but all the people born in the wilderness during the journey from Egypt had not. The Israelites had moved about in the desert forty years until all the men who were of military age when they left Egypt had died, since they had not obeyed the Lord. For the Lord had sworn to them that they would not see the land he had solemnly promised their ancestors to give us, a land flowing with milk and honey. So he raised up their sons in their place, and these were the ones Joshua circumcised. They were still uncircumcised because they had not been circumcised on the way. And after the whole nation had been circumcised, they remained where they were in camp until they were healed."

In other words, God does this because He had a covenant with Abraham. It is because of this covenant that we see that circumcision provided a physical reminder that Israel was to have faith in God's promise that declared they were to become a fruitful nation. God was to be their God, and He would look after their future generations. Circumcision stood as a physical reminder that they had a covenant with God that called them to follow Him by faith, and that He in turn would provide for them.

Also, before they do anything else, they observe Passover. Passover reminds them of what happened in Egypt. It is as if God knows they may start to doubt Him, and so in an attempt to build their faith, He has them circumcised and reminds them of the covenant, and then they partake in Passover, which reminds them of what Christ did in freeing their parents from slavery in Egypt. This is also probably why God dries up the Jordan. It is as if He is telling them: "Just as I was with your fathers in Egypt crossing the Red Sea, so I will be with you now." And also: "Just as we overcame the Egyptians, so will we overcome the people of Canaan."

You see, God is preparing them for Jericho, and they don't even know it yet! And this is why my biggest recommendation to you in your worship time is to not just read devotionals that talk about God, but read the Bible for yourself. If one morning you are running behind on time and you have only 10 minutes, by all means, put down my book and pick up His. My book, while useful (if I do say so myself), is not going to radically change your life. Only His can do that. Pairing the two is my suggestion. The Bible is so intentional and filled with so many incredible applications that it is mind-blowing. When you start to actually read the Bible and try to understand why it paints a certain picture, God will become real to you, because everything on those pages was put there intentionally. God is incredibly thoughtful. Remember this in your own life. God doesn't bring you to something without first preparing you for the mission.

Now they are ready to hear about God's plans for Jericho. We read in Joshua 5:13-15, "Now when Joshua was near Jericho, he looked up and saw a man standing in front of him with a drawn sword in his hand. Joshua went up to him and asked, 'Are you for us or for our enemies?' 'Neither,' he replied, 'but as commander of the army of the Lord I have now come.' Then Joshua fell facedown to the ground in reverence, and asked him, 'What message does my Lord have for his servant?' The commander of the Lord's army replied, 'Take off your sandals, for the place where you are standing is holy.' And Joshua did so."

Again we see God's thoughtfulness. Why would God appear to Joshua with a sword drawn? When you read the Bible, start asking yourself "Why?" over every line, and you will have a better understanding of just how incredible Christ is. Christ standing before Joshua, sword drawn, is meant to encourage Joshua. It's as if Christ is saying, "Oh, did you think you were heading into this battle alone? No, Joshua. I will be heading into the battle with you. We are in this thing together. My sword is already drawn."

Two other things I would like to note here from this chapter. First, when God speaks to us or sends angels to speak to us, they come in the form of the person they are speaking with. God must have looked similar to the Israelites as well, because Joshua asked him, "Are you for us or for our enemies?" I want to note that just because the Bible is completed, we think God no longer deals with us directly. Scripture tells us plainly that just as Joshua did, you too may have encountered a heavenly visitor.

Hebrews 13:2 says, "Do not forget to show hospitality to strangers, for by so doing some people have shown hospitality to angels without knowing it."

The writing of the Bible is completed, but your story isn't. God is still using you, watching you, and molding you into the person He needs to accomplish the task you were created for. God may send an angel to deal with you or test you on some issue. And when He does, don't expect to see a being with a robe of light and six wings. Expect to see someone who makes you feel comfortable and seems very similar to you. In other words, you probably will never know the heavenly encounter you just had, unless, for whatever reason, God reveals it to you.

The second thing I want to note from Joshua 5 is that the angel of the Lord tells Joshua to remove his sandals because he is on holy ground. This tells us that Joshua is meeting with Christ, because He repeats to him words similar to those He spoke to Moses in Exodus 3:5. You see, when in the presence of God, you are on holy ground. It is with this reverence that we should come to God in prayer, and with this attitude that we should seek Him in Scripture. God is holy, and with nothing but reverence should you seek His Spirit.

Next we read in Joshua 6:1-5, "Now the gates of Jericho were securely barred because of the Israelites. No one went out and no one came in. Then the Lord said to Joshua, 'See, I have delivered Jericho into your hands, along with its king and its fighting men. March around the city once with all the armed men. Do this for six days. Have seven priests carry trumpets of rams' horns in front of the ark. On the seventh day, march around the city seven times, with the priests blowing the trumpets. When you hear them sound a long blast on the trumpets, have the whole army give a loud shout; then the wall of the city will collapse and the army will go up, everyone straight in.'"

Now, I am sure the Israelites are a bit confused by God's command, but remember, He has just spent a great deal of time renewing their faith. They are ready to do as He asks because they have remembered what He has done in the past, and they have renewed their own covenant with Him.

Now, the people of Jericho probably got a good laugh out of watching the Israelites march around their city for six days. "Surely they don't think walking around the walls will win them a battle," I'm sure they joked with one another.

I'd also like to note that each time they marched around the city, they did so in complete silence. They needed silence, because God was working and sowing seeds of faith in their hearts. How many times do you think you have corrupted a blessing sent by God because you were unable to sit still, be silent, and let His hand work?

On the seventh day, with nothing but blares from their trumpet horns and shouts to heaven from the base of their lungs, God stretched out His mighty hand and delivered the city to them.

I love how God left them with absolutely no doubt about just whose victory was won. Had they climbed the walls, penetrated the city, then slew the inhabitants, I think it would have been easy for many of them to gain pride in the work of their own hands, much like hundreds of years later would be the mistake of their first king, Saul. Instead, God destroyed the once-notorious walls of Jericho using nothing but the decibels in their voices as He responded to their cries of deliverance.

When I was a child, that was always where the story ended, with God's victory and the Israelites' great testament of faith. Imagine my surprise as a young adult searching through Scripture on my own accord and discovering that that was not where the story of Jericho ended at all. Because this victory was not theirs, but God's, a proclamation had gone out that all the spoils of the city would be given in a sacrifice to Jehovah. All the silver, gold, bronze, and iron was to be brought to the Lord's treasury.

They were instructed that every living thing, sparing the life of Rahab and her family, was to be destroyed. They were to destroy everything, even the strongest oxen, the best food, the most fertile cattle—all of that was to be devoured in flames as acknowledgment of their Deliverer. After all, they had done nothing by which they should preserve the treasures for themselves. This victory was God's, and He even did it in a way that none among them could assume otherwise.

Not long after their defeat of Jericho, the confident Israelites set out to also demolish the city of Ai. With the leadership of Joshua and their newfound faith in Christ, they were certain that this too would be an easy victory. They sent 3,000 men in to bring down the city, and imagine their dismay as the warriors of Ai disbanded these confident men, who had just witnessed the hand of God in Jericho. Some men died, others ran, but the multitudes of Israelites were left confused and disheartened.

In anguish Joshua cried out to God, questioning why He would bring them this far, only to suffer defeat. God, who had found favor in Joshua early on, responded to him that he needed to check with his people, because someone's sin was hindering their victory. Someone in the camp of Israel had ignored the command and kept some of the spoils from Jericho. In secret, when no one was watching, they had succumbed to temptation, forgetting that with the God of heaven and earth there are no secrets.

Ellen White writes in *Patriarchs and Prophets*, "Early in the morning, Joshua gathered the people together by their tribes, and the solemn and impressive ceremony began. Step by step the investigation went on. Closer and still closer came the fearful test. First the tribe, then the family, then the household, then the man was taken, and Achan the son of Carmi, of the tribe of Judah, was pointed out by the finger of God as the troubler of Israel. . . . [And] 'all Israel stoned him with stones.' Then there was raised over him a great pile of stones—a witness to the sin and its punishment" (p. 495).

Achan's secret sin held back the entire people of Israel from their victory in Ai. For his desire of a Babylonian garment, men lost their lives. Even as the ceremony was taking place, Achan clearly attempted and hoped to conceal his sin further. How long would it have taken to go through an entire multitude of people? How many hours did Achan have to confess his sin, even after discovering that it was because of his sin that the first battle against Ai was lost? His heart worried only for himself, and clearly he was not stricken with regret or a need to confess in hopes of forgiveness until he knew he had absolutely no way out and had been called on by name and selected by the finger of God.

In truth, this is the story that relates most closely to our own lives. We have moments in life like the battle of Jericho, where we stand with faith, and with God's aid are able to do the impossible. We have spiritual highs, during which we move mountains, slay giants, or bring down city walls with nothing but conviction in our voice. In honesty, those moments of victory are often overshadowed with secret sins that we've managed to disguise as goodly treasure. Oftentimes we never confess. We conceal them and bury them further till, like the Israelites in their first battle at Ai, we have hindered our prayers or our efforts from any further victory.

Instead of searching inward to seek out the cause of our misfortune, we blame God. "How could You do this to me?" we cry, and often not in silence.

I was a young girl the first time I discussed with my father some matter I was bringing to the Lord and not feeling any resolve.

"He is not listening to me," I told him.

"What could be hindering your prayers?" he responded.

I didn't really get it. I was young and arrogant, and assumed that surely I had done enough in my life to be keeping God happy. The second I finished reading the story of Jericho on my own, without taking anyone else's word for what happened, I fully understood.

What Babylonian garment is currently buried in your closet? What secrets are you keeping that may be hindering your prayers? Who knows, had Achan confessed his sin outright, he may have been spared. Let the pile of stones that once covered his body serve as a symbol for you in your life that Achan's death was not in vain. Let his story change the course of your own.

Surely, for now, we can all hide. But a day will come when tribe by tribe, household by household, one by one, we will stand in the presence of Jesus Christ to answer for the things we have done in public and in secret. Don't wait for that moment to confess out of fear rather than redemption. Let no secret desire, no jealous nature, no hate or anger or guilt, keep you from gaining one more victory.

Reflection: "Have mercy on me, O God, according to your unfailing love; according to your great compassion blot out my transgressions" (Psalm 51:1).

Day 11

"I just want to go through Central Park and watch folks passing by. Spend the whole day watching people. I miss that."
—Barack Obama

I was in the fifth or sixth grade the first time I overheard the conversation that put the leash around my neck that would bind my future with literature.

"Well, you know what they say," a girl said to her classmate with a smile on her face. "If you ever want to hide something from a Black man, just put it in a book."

I now honestly cannot even remember the face of the girl who said it, nor do I remember the face of her giggling comrade. I do know that my mouth became dry. I was very unfamiliar with racism. My tiny town did a good job of shielding me from ignorant comments for most of my life. There are people from every race in the town of Berrien Springs. I always meet people who tell me otherwise, that their experience here was much different from my own. Perhaps I was just so stuck in my own imaginary worlds I didn't really notice what was going on in the real one. I do remember this incident, though; it ripped through my daydreams, and I was never the same after. I'm not sure if it was defensiveness that plagued me, or if it was that, for a moment, I was worried it was true. I felt my tongue swell within my jaws as I suddenly craved a sip of water. Panic will make you thirsty—must be something about the rush of adrenaline.

I let her words marinate on my ears as I hid behind a locker in that hallway, hoping they wouldn't notice me. I tucked those words away. I put them on my soul like a tattoo that could never be erased. I branded myself with that phrase, and from then on I wore it. I dressed myself in it during conversations and let it lay on me like a tightly fitted suit. Even still, as I rise in the morning, I make sure to put it on. I need it now. It reminds me of who I am and where I came from. It showed me that a quick word without thought can smudge someone else's hope and leave them changed. Had I not had such powerful and inspirational Black figures right in my own family, I could have found myself believing them. I was lucky, though, because I already knew the truth: skin does not have the power of hiding things from people; people have to choose to hide things from themselves.

Later that day, as I walked down the hallways to class, I left trails of my childhood inside that school. I decided not to tell my White mother or Black father what I had overheard that day, and I also never asked them whether or not it was true, although, I did decide on one thing: No one would ever hide anything from me. I wouldn't allow it. And I didn't. I read every book that I could find—books about topics that pulled me into another person's shoes, and books that really didn't interest me at all. I am probably one of the only sixth graders who ordered their own copy of *A Tale of Two Cities*, Charles Dickens' 1859 classic, and memorized his most famous paragraph: "It was the best of times, it was the worst of times." Reading became my passageway into myself.

Yes, God put me in that hallway for the same reason He's put you exactly where you are at this moment while you're reading through my words. Listening is learning, and people are knowledge. Good or bad, we can learn from one another. It is a hefty weight to bear, knowing that a few careless words when you think no one hears you can permanently be burned into someone else's eardrums and change the way they see themselves and the world around them. Perhaps that is why I wanted to start writing, to work on undoing some of the damage others more careless than I had done. Perhaps my words can erase the memory of someone else's. The number one reason you hear from secular society regarding why they no longer attend church is often similar to Gandhi's evaluation of Christianity when he said, "I like your Christ; I do not like your Christians. Your Christians are so unlike your Christ."

It was God's plan that the Israelites were to enter the Promised Land shortly after leaving Egypt. Because of a lack of faith and constant rebellion, He condemns them to wander the desert for 40 years, and most of them die there. He raises up a new generation, and with that generation acting on faith, He allows them to enter the Promised Land. So here is the question: Could spiritual Israel (the Christian church after Jesus, in Matthew 28:19, 20, commissioned the disciples to take His message to all ends of the earth), because of lack of faith, rebellion, and a lack of love for one another, which is what Jesus spent a great deal of effort preaching about in His three-year ministry, also be experiencing a delay in His second coming? When the people don't meet the standards, God changes the plan and waits for a generation that is ready for the task. Spiritual Israel has hundreds if not thousands of applications that can be made while reading about the literal Israelites. Could this be one of them?

What do you think? Could we be delaying Christ's return? In one of Jesus' last prayers to His Father before the Crucifixion, He says in John 17:11, "I will remain in the world no longer, but they are still in the world, and I am coming to you. Holy Father, protect them by the power of your name, the name you gave me," and then He utters the line that I think is utterly important: "so that they may be one as we are one." Jesus prayed and acted as the intercessor before His crucifixion by asking that we become one just as He and the Father are one. Jesus wants unity, but are we united? Are we one?

This generation may be leaving the church at alarming rates, but they are hungry and thirsty for community. This generation wants authentic Christian relationships. This generation, perhaps unlike the generation before them, is seeking to become one, and so Satan, in an attempt to mess things up, starts separating them from the church. I don't know about you, but I am tired of wandering. I want to enter the Promised Land. I want to do my part to stop this delay.

I used to feel very comfortable on this earth. I used to feel very connected to my life here, and, if I am being honest, when I prayed for Christ to return, I wasn't sure if I meant it. I watched a movie with my husband that changed my life. It's called *The Stoning of Soraya*. It is a true story about a stoning committed in the mid-1980s in a rural Arab town. After watching that film, I realized that while I am comfortable, many others are not. If I love my brothers and sisters, I should be praying for their deliverance. Also, I cannot love my life and the people surrounding me more than I love Christ. Isn't this why Adam fell, for his love of Eve?

If I do not want to see the face of my sweet Savior more than anything else, then I am disconnected. The only pause I should be petitioning Christ for is more time to finish my job as a facilitator of His good news. For that, I need more time. He and I both know that there is a great job to be done, and many hands make light work. For that, I am so happy that you and I have met. Revival is sure to come, because you are God's next big thing.

It is my own personal belief that people are a lot like books. Every day they pass me by in the hundreds, enough walking books to make any one of us brilliant. Each face is concealing the most intriguing of stories. When we ignore people, when we don't listen to the messages they are trying desperately to send us, we've lost pages of a story that could have deeply impacted our own. Don't let your own ignorance cause these walking treasures to be hidden from you.

The beauty and brilliance I encounter by meeting people never ceases to amaze me. Not just passing them, but by actually meeting people. The second I meet people, the second I get behind the face and into the soul, I'm almost always impressed. People are all so unique and different, and even if I don't agree with everything, I can often find pieces or elements of who they are that inspire me. You find out that the gorgeous girl with the flawless hair studied martial arts, or that the perfect boy with the cookie-cutter family was molested when he was 5. Everyone has a story to tell, and I like to be well-read.

What is the most frustrating to me is how we turn off each other's messages because we don't appreciate the packaging it comes in. I always watch in dismay at the bookstore as people put down great pieces of literature because they don't like the cover. One of my absolute best reads of all time is *The Glass Castle*. The cover is plain. You'd never know that the pages contain one of the most captivating true stories of struggle and perseverance I've ever read.

In the same light, we lose something when we ignore one another because we don't like the clothes that we are seeing. We can't identify with the weight they are, the teeth they have, the color of their skin, and so we simply turn them off. We quickly disregard them, and then continue praying to God for answers to various questions. Little did we know that they were the answer, that within their story was a piece of our story, a line of common ground that we could have understood. That had we just spoken to them or listened to them, we would have seen that we aren't alone in this world, and that people, people much like the ones we just passed, are in our paths for a reason. Instead of figuring out those reasons, we throw them over our shoulders much like we'd chuck a penny into a fountain.

It is my belief that the most inspirational and educational gifts God gave us to help navigate through life are other people. Every great writer knows that their creative genius is dependent upon how much reading they do themselves, because great reading inspires even better writing. In the same way, your story becomes all the more enriching and beautiful the second you take the time to listen to and read the person sitting right next to you.

Reflection: "Hatred stirs up conflict, but love covers over all wrongs" (Proverbs 10:12).

Day 12

"Faith isn't faith until it's all you're holding on to."
—P.B.S. Pinchback

I was sitting at my dining room table a few mornings ago. I was running a little farther behind schedule than I would have liked, and for a few moments I contemplated skipping my morning Bible read and going straight to prayer. Every time I think of doing that, though, my mind flashes back to a sermon by Pastor Esther Knott in which she recounted a collegiate memory when a professor asked her, "What did you learn from your Scripture reading today?" She didn't know how to respond, because that particular morning she hadn't read anything. She wanted to make sure that this never happened to her again. We should be taking in Scripture every day. It is how we grow spiritually. So though I pondered skipping my read, I thought about that question, "What did you learn from your Scripture reading today?" and I was reminded that I must be able to provide an answer to that question every day.

I am currently in Isaiah. My Bible reading strategy is simple. As with every other book, I start it from the beginning and read it all the way through. The only difference is that unlike other books, once I am finished I start over. It's amazing how infinite the Bible is. No matter how many times you read the same chapters, new things seem to strike you depending on where you are at in your life. Lines that once were seemingly insignificant suddenly become highlighted because my life has changed, and, therefore, so has my perspective.

The other morning I read about King Hezekiah being ill and at the point of death. In Isaiah 38:1 he receives word from the prophet Isaiah about his circumstances. It reads, "This is what the Lord says: Put your house in order, because you are going to die; you will not recover."

It continues in verses 2 and 3: "Hezekiah turned his face to the wall and prayed to the Lord, 'Remember, Lord, how I have walked before you faithfully and with wholehearted devotion and have done what is good in your eyes.' And Hezekiah wept bitterly." In verses 5 and 6 God answers Hezekiah's prayer. He tells the prophet, "Go and tell Hezekiah, 'This is what the Lord, the God of your father David, says: I have heard your prayer and seen your tears; I will add fifteen years to your life. And I will deliver you and this city from the hand of the king of Assyria. I will defend this city.'"

Naturally, I was struck by the power of prayer in this story. Hezekiah prayed one of the most trying prayers; he asked to be spared while in the face of death. God heard his prayer and spared his life for another 15 years. While reading that story, I found it revitalizing. I pray every day, so sometimes I can't help getting caught in routine. I like when I am reminded that prayer is powerful and that God is listening, and sometimes gives us the answers we hope to hear.

When I sit here now reflecting on that story, I cannot help thinking of my husband. I am sure he prayed a prayer similar to Hezekiah's in the intercession for his brother Tyler, who was diagnosed with cancer while still trying to complete eighth grade. Tyler did live to finish high school, but died shortly after that. Oftentimes, as I sit and pray earnestly for my own child, I think about the prayers, the tears, and the sleepless nights my mother-in-law must have gone through.

Right now, in my womb, rests a beautiful baby girl for whom I pray incessantly for God's protection. It's hard to reconcile this idea that Tyler, who was also my mother-in-law's firstborn, and for whom I'm sure she spent many days and nights praying incessantly, would later be stricken with such a terrible disease. When we speak of it now, she tells me that heaven is tangible for her, because heaven isn't a question mark; it has a face. Heaven is Tyler.

When Christ returns, the saints that have passed away will rise, and in the air she will be brought together with the face that could have, had she allowed it, destroyed her faith, but instead kept her focused on the true meaning of this life. In her words I find immense faith, a level of faith that I pray I myself can find. Probably one of the greatest testaments of faith I have ever seen, I have seen in her eyes. There really is nothing like the heart of a mother, voice shaken, faith tested and bruised, pained by the memory of the loss of her son, and yet joyful because she knows that in heaven her family will be restored. When the grave bursts open, Tyler won't be sick, but will be made perfect in mind, body, and spirit. She believes that, and that is faith.

When I started writing this entry, I meant to express to you the power of prayer. As often happens, through writing I am reminded that prayer alone means nothing; it's faith that defines true patriarchs. We talk a lot about prayer as Christians, because prayer is easy. Anyone can toss words to God throughout their day. It is really faith that must permeate that prayer in order for true reformation. When we have faith that it is Christ whom we are addressing, it will change the way we pray to Him. When we have faith that He actually has a plan, the only plan, it will change the way we accept His responses. Faith is the key to prayer. Faith in His plan is the key to getting through this life.

I was struck by the words in Isaiah 37:35, which say, "I will defend this city and save it, for my sake and for the sake of David my servant!" Now, David had been long gone, but it was because of him that Christ often spared Israel. David was a man of not only soulful prayer but also iconic faith. When all of Israel trembled at the size of Goliath, the boy David saw only a chance to prove just how big his God was. When he sinned and God offered him the chance to pick his punishment, it was with faith in Christ's character that David responded.

Second Samuel 24:12-16 reads, "Go and tell David, 'This is what the Lord says: I am giving you three options. Choose one of them for me to carry out against you.' So Gad went to David and said to him, 'Shall there come on you three years of famine in your land? Or three months of fleeing from your enemies while they pursue you? Or three days of plague in your land? Now then, think it over and decide how I should answer the one who sent me.' David said to Gad, 'I am in deep distress. Let us fall into the hands of the Lord, for his mercy is great; but do not let me fall into human hands.' So the Lord sent a plague on Israel from that morning until the end of the time designated, and seventy thousand of the people from Dan to Beersheba died. When the angel stretched out his hand to destroy Jerusalem, the Lord relented concerning the disaster and said to the angel who was afflicting the people, 'Enough! Withdraw your hand.' The angel of the Lord was then at the threshing floor of Araunah the Jebusite."

And it is there on the threshing floor of Araunah the Jebusite that David built an altar in honor of the God who punishes sin, but not without mercy. David's faith in God's character influenced his decisions, and God showed mercy. Ezekiel 18:23 says, "Do I take any pleasure in the death of the wicked? declares the Sovereign Lord. Rather, am I not pleased when they turn from their ways and live?" God does not take pleasure in even the death of those who deserve it, so how much more would He mourn for those of us who meet it with pureness of heart? We must, through faith, remember that this world, though significant to us, serves only one purpose to Christ: to allow us to either accept or reject Him. Heaven is where life starts.

At first when I read Isaiah 38, I thought the point was that prayer is power. Now, as I reread it with my new perspective, I recognize the real rock of Hezekiah's prayer. "Remember, Lord, how I have walked before you faithfully and with wholehearted devotion" (verse 3). Hezekiah was not just a man of great prayer; he was also a man of proven faith. It wasn't because of his prayer that Hezekiah was granted recovery from his illness; it was because of his faith, and how he had served God faithfully. Yes, prayer creates power, but faith creates discipleship.

Reflection: "I keep my eyes always on the Lord. With him at my right hand, I will not be shaken" (Psalm 16:8).

Day 13

"First we make our habits, then our habits make us."
—Charles C. Noble

When I was younger, after I recognized that singing was not my avenue, I wanted to be an actress. In the fourth grade my teacher, Mrs. Ingrid Moon, wanted to foster my creativity so that it did not disturb her classroom. She allowed me to write skits, rehearse during recesses; and on Fridays I'd perform them for the entire class. Looking back now, I feel extremely grateful to her and to other teachers who allowed me my creative freedom. It's remarkable that she would allow me that five, or so, minutes every Friday to present a skit. She took what others saw as weakness, an overactive imagination without purpose, and she gave it direction.

Sometimes I'd be a one-man band; other times I'd hold auditions for roles and try to encourage my classmates to take part. I can remember being terribly upset if they did not take their roles in our dramas seriously. Recess was not a time for tag or catch; it was rehearsal. I was such a strange child. However, I was motivated. I loved writing, and I liked being up front, so why couldn't I be an actress?

Looking back on my childhood, I can't help smiling about some of the aspects of my personality that have just been ingrained in my DNA. Then there are so many other pieces that make up who I am that I really don't like. I am opinionated and stubborn, not traits that our society particularly finds attractive in females. I can honestly say that I am truly blessed. I think my best qualities are really just reflections of the parenting done by my mother and father. My mom and dad were incredible parents to me. Looking back, there is really nothing different I wish they had done.

I attended a Bible study led by my friend Cortney a couple weeks ago. The topic she selected was forgiveness and how the Bible would have you deal with it. Immediately when she told me the topic I thought to myself, *Well, this is nice; maybe my husband can get something out of it.*

My point is that my immediate thought was that this study was not going to relate to me. I've never had an issue with forgiveness. My typical style is that I get really angry, vent for a couple days, and then I am over it. I honestly can't really think of one person I am currently holding a grudge against, or ever have for that matter. Sure, people have said things to hurt me, done things that disappointed me, but I've never carried it with me long after the event.

Sometimes I wish I could hold a grudge. I hate when I am trying to be mad at my husband for whatever dumb thing he did that I can nag him about this week, and then without warning he apologizes. We can be arguing, I can be steaming mad, and suddenly, at the height of my anger, he will throw his hands in the air and relent. "You're right; I'm sorry," he says, and then moves in for some physical form of affection that lets him know I am moving on. In those moments, sometimes I want to stay mad. I am not done complaining. But when he looks at me and pulls me in, I melt. I want to revel in "mad Heather time," but he said he was sorry, he is pulling me in, and so I just can't.

Cortney opened the Bible study by asking if there was ever a time someone really let us down that still haunts us and we can't seem to get over. Again, I thought to myself, *Nope, not me*, because forgiveness wasn't my problem. I looked at my husband as if to signal that I hoped he was paying attention. Seth knows how to hold a grudge.

She quoted such texts as Matthew 5:22-24, which says, "'But I tell you that anyone who is angry with a brother or sister will be subject to judgment. Again, anyone who says to a brother or sister, 'Raca,' is answerable to the court. And anyone who says, 'You fool!' will be in danger of the fire of hell. Therefore, if you are offering your gift at the altar and there remember that your brother or sister has something against you, leave your gift there in front of the altar. First go and be reconciled to them; then come and offer your gift."

She also used the story of Jesus speaking to the accusers and the woman caught in adultery. Luke 7:47, 48, which says: "'Therefore, I tell you, her many sins have been forgiven—as her great love has shown. But whoever has been forgiven little loves little.' Then Jesus said to her, 'Your sins are forgiven.'"

And last, 2 Corinthians 5:18, 19: "All this is from God, who reconciled us to himself through Christ and gave us the ministry of reconciliation: that God was reconciling the world to himself in Christ, not counting people's sins against them. And he has committed to us the message of reconciliation."

She shared these verses, and I looked over at my husband to make sure he was getting them. You see, this was a Bible study for him, not me, and so I saw the value in her words and wanted to make sure he was processing this valuable insight. Suddenly a thought struck me: *Maybe the only reason forgiveness isn't my problem is because nothing so terrible has ever happened to me that has tested my forgiveness.*

I thought about people I know who were molested by family members they trusted, and the painful scars that this has left on their lives.

I thought about my husband, who lost his brother to cancer when he was 17 years old, and I realized how that could make a person angry. I looked at Cortney, who had tears in her eyes as she shared a story about someone who had betrayed her. I thought about the portfolio journals I had read from my students, one of them saying she had been molested by her stepdad from the time she was 7 till she finally told someone when she was 17. I thought about the real reasons people hold grudges. I thought about the real issue with forgiveness, when it is simply too painful.

I looked back at my husband, and I thought, *If he was to cheat on me, could I honestly forgive him for that?* I thought about my daughter and wondered, *If someone was to hurt her, could I forgive them?*

To be honest, I wasn't sure of the answer to any of those questions, and I'm still not. If I had suffered sexual abuse, forgiveness would be hard for me. If my husband disrespected me and our family with infidelity, I really think the hate that would enter my heart for him would create a huge wedge in my personal and spiritual life that I am not sure I would be able to remove. And I cannot even think about a hair on my daughter's head being put out of place. Forgiveness hasn't been my issue, because my life is full of spilled milk, not actual turmoil that some people deal with.

I realized, at this point in my life, I am the most spiritually connected to Christ I have ever been, ever, and yet if something severe happened, I honestly am not sure how I would react to it. Forgiveness isn't my problem—yet. If I want to reflect Christ fully, I need to prepare my heart to meet the bad as well as the good.

Oftentimes I meet people who have these incredibly tumultuous pasts. In some ways I envy them. My mother-in-law, for example, is one of the most inspiring women I have ever met. Her story is not my story to tell, but I look at the beautiful woman she is in spite of various trials, and I am left awed. Her intact faith after the loss of her first child honestly moves me to tears. My sister-in-law also inspires me. She's encountered more adversity than most could handle watching in a movie, and yet she trusts in Christ.

When I say I envy them, I mean that the writer in me sometimes wishes that I had an incredible story of peaks and valleys such as theirs to share with the world. People would read their stories and think, *If she can do it, I can do it.* I, however, have no powerful story of struggle. My parents were exceptional, my husband is incredible, and my grandparents are precious, right down to my exceedingly supportive aunts and uncles. I have really had every opportunity in life to succeed.

I think about that sometimes, and I wonder, *If everyone around me has been so perfect to me and I have reaped every benefit from having such supportive and loving figures in my life, even down to the teachers who allowed me to perform skits in their classes, why am I so far from perfection?* I have no testimony of true hardship. In fact, I grew up in a home in which Christ was reflected to me daily. They all did their part. I had every opportunity to live a life that would prove stronger than Satan's temptations, and yet I am so blemished it's pathetic.

Sometimes the only thing harder than having someone or some circumstance to blame for your own imperfections is having no one to blame but yourself. That is a hard truth for me to swallow, the truth that I am unworthy of God's affection, and by my own accord. It's like in my childhood dramas: I'm still a one-man band, only this time I am not acting. The devil is clever, because as you contemplate sin he minimizes it.

"It's not that big of a deal," he whispers in your ear. "So you did it one time—so what?" He tempts you by minimizing the choice, and then the second you make it, he turns on you. He pummels you with guilt and weighs you down with regret. The very same sin he first minimized, he then uses to separate you from God. And when it is all over and you look around for the trigger, someone to blame for why you are feeling the way you are now, the room is empty. The stage is dark except for your shadow and the spotlight beaming on your silhouette.

Don't let the devil achieve his most prized objective. Sure, he wants you to sin, but even more than that, he wants you to allow the guilt to separate you from Christ. He wants you to end up like he is; he wants company in his banishment. There is no sin too great for God's mercy. Even when there is no one else to blame, God wants nothing more than to swoop in and wipe you clean. He is a Savior. You must allow Him to be who He instinctively is. He did not die on a cross for a world too lost for His mercy. He died to give mercy to a world that would otherwise be lost.

So maybe you're like many others with a story of heartache that keeps holding you back from truly connecting with Christ. Or maybe you are like me, with the only villain in your story being yourself. Forgiveness is essential, because if we cannot forgive others, how can we expect God to forgive us?

In my own life, I can forgive others, but I must also learn to forgive myself.

Either way, the same holds true: We cannot rewrite the past, but we can start today scripting our future. Trust me, the best part about being a writer is that it is never too late to give yourself a happy ending.

Reflection: "He has shown you, O mortal, what is good. And what does the Lord require of you? To act justly and to love mercy and to walk humbly with your God" (Micah 6:8).

Day 14

If you haven't noticed yet, I absolutely adore my husband. He is the best thing that has ever happened to me. Sometimes when I wake up in the morning, I lie in bed for a few moments just daydreaming about our first date, or first kiss, or the day he asked me to marry him. He put a lot of thought and energy into his proposal to me, and remembering it makes me smile.

Before I explain how he proposed, I first have to give a little preface into my passions. I love to write. I even love the way my pen feels as I curl my fingers over it as if to guard my most precious instrument. A pen is an instrument really. It's a writer's piano. In the wrong hands it can play an awful pitch. But in the hands of a cautious musician, you can hear symphonies. My pen has always played me melodies.

Some writers feel that their instruments may get out of tune. They can write only in certain places and areas with strategically placed objects. Many writers, for example, have to be in a quiet room—just them and the keyboard. Others have a set routine. They write only at night with the lights off, a window opened, and a glass of chardonnay an arm's reach away. I, however, can write anywhere.

As a child I wrote poems and songs before I fell asleep. In high school I wrote short stories outdoors. If it was winter, I'd open the blinds and press my body as close to God's nature as I could get without the snow directly falling above me. I'd clutch my piano between my fingers, and always keep a hot cup of cocoa or cider beside me. In college I wrote in class. My professors all thought I was an avid note taker as my eyes glazed and my back hunched over my white paper with blue letters sprinkled like seeds across it. I finished my first novel that way, perhaps explaining why I was no longer an A student.

The only thing I love just as much as writing is reading. Reading is part of what opens my brain to writing. I don't just read books; I get lost in them. I love painting in the faces for the heroes and villains that I meet while reading. It's like a movie that plays in your mind. My husband is an excellent carpenter, and he keeps promising that my next present will be a handmade bookshelf. I can't wait to get that gift, because then I can place my favorite books on a shelf built by his hands, and that will be priceless.

When my husband proposed to me, it was Christmas Eve. I knew he was going to propose at some point, because we had been talking very seriously about marriage. On the first date I had with my husband, he told me he didn't think he would ever get married. Then when we had been dating for about a year, he said that we would get married, but he wasn't rushing anything. Then, very suddenly, he told me that not only did he want to get married, but that he wanted to get married right away. It literally seemed to happen overnight, and I'm not sure what switches flipped in his brain that made him suddenly so sure of everything, but I was happy he was. So daily he had been telling me that he wanted to marry me, so I was just waiting for him to finally make it official with his proposal.

We were going to his parents' house an hour and a half away for Christmas Eve dinner, so he had told me the night before he wanted to exchange gifts in the afternoon. I wondered if he would have a ring for me, but when I got home I saw he had a bunch of presents, so I figured it wasn't likely. The next week was my birthday anyway, so I thought maybe he was waiting to ask me then. After I opened the 10 or so presents he had wrapped for me (none of which was a ring), he pulled out one more that he had left behind my tree. The second I looked at it, I could tell it was a book. I was happy, because I love people getting me thoughtful gifts, and the idea of him strumming through a bookstore trying to find a book he thought I'd like was precious.

When I opened the last present, it was a book, but not the type of book I was hoping for. It was one of those Old-English-literature-classic-type books with 2,000-plus pages. Something like Mark Twain would have put together. I appreciated the thought, and I tried to pretend to be excited, but on the inside I was thinking that these were not the types of books I enjoyed reading leisurely.

"Do you like it?" he asked.

"Love it!" I lied.

"Well, it's kind of an old book. There is a special way to read it; let me show you," he said, taking the book from me and holding it firmly in his hands. Once he opened the book, he flipped the pages together fast, the way you would with those old picture books that show a stickman, and as you flip them you see him running. On the corner of each page he had put a letter, so when you flipped the pages fast it formed the words "Will You Marry Me?" In the back of the book he had cut out a hole in the pages and put a beautiful solitaire diamond ring.

I was so happy. Not only because he had just asked me to marry him, but also because he had done it in a way that would mean something special to me. I loved to write and I loved to read, and so he had asked me to enter into a world with him by first entering mine. It was incredibly thoughtful, a good reflection of his character. So sometimes when I wake up in the morning, I stay in bed a few extra moments and reflect on things like that. Precious memories that are held tightly in my mind and make my heart swell because I love him so much.

The other day, after lying in bed a few extra moments thinking about Seth, I wondered if I give God as much love and adoration as I give my husband. I am madly in love with Seth, and I wondered if I am equally as madly in love with Christ. Don't get me wrong; I love God and am passionate about Him. My favorite conversations are those in which people bring up His name, but do I wake up every day thinking about how good He is? Do I suddenly smile out of nowhere because a thought of Him enters my mind?

I am so glad God placed Seth in my life, because He has given me an excellent example of what my relationship with Him should be like. When I think about leaving work to come home to Seth, I smile. Sometimes it is that thought that gets me through a rough day. When something goes wrong, when someone hurts me, when I fail, when I make a mistake, I call Seth. When something goes well, when I get a promotion, when I receive a letter from someone who was touched by a book or magazine article I wrote, when I have a good run, read a good book, make a good dish of food, I can't wait to call Seth, show Seth, set Seth down and ask him to just guess what happened to me that day. My husband is my world, and I think that is great, but it also reminds me that my number one relationship has to be with God, or else I am just almost there, and almost doesn't count.

The Bible often refers to our relationship with God being like a marriage. We should be committed, in love, and in tune with God, much like the ingredients we would need to be married. If I were being completely honest, I would say that in my current spiritual life, I am dating God. We are going strong, and I think we may even get engaged soon. You see, my goal is marriage. My goal is complete devotion and utter commitment.

When I think of biblical role models for what I want my relationship with God to be like one day, I think of Samuel and David. I am in love with Christ, but I don't want to just be in love with Him; I want to marry Him. What makes the difference between just being in love with someone and marrying them? I think it's commitment, commitment to putting the work into the relationship to meet your mutual goals.

As I was thinking about all this, I was reminded of Christ's charge to the disciples as He was providing them with the information they would need to set forth and create the Christian church. First He lets them know that it is not going to be easy. He tells them they will be hunted, persecuted, beaten, and worn, but that He will provide them with words to speak and with His Spirit. He tells them that He has already numbered the hairs on their head and that they should not be afraid.

Toward the end of His instructions we see Him say this in Matthew 10:37-39: "Anyone who loves their father or mother more than me is not worthy of me; anyone who loves their son or daughter more than me is not worthy of me. Whoever does not take up their cross and follow me is not worthy of me. Whoever finds their life will lose it, and whoever loses their life for my sake will find it."

You cannot place any relationship over your relationship with Christ. And so if you have been blessed with extreme love in your life as I have, use that relationship as your measuring tool. I love Seth dearly, and so I have to make sure I am that much more in love with God. This is important, in my opinion, because the whole reason the earth fell was that Adam placed his need for an earthly companion higher than His spiritual connection. When the Ten Commandments say to honor your father and mother, it is not just because they are your elders, but also because if you can't respect those who you can see, how can you respect someone you cannot see? God doesn't take second place, and if He comes in second, you are not worthy of Him. You must marry Christ.

Where is your current relationship with God? In the end, when all is said and done, will "dating" Him be enough? Will He be satisfied with that? He shouldn't be, and we shouldn't be either.

Reflection: "As a young man marries a young woman, so will your Builder marry you; as a bridegroom rejoices over his bride, so will your God rejoice over you" (Isaiah 62:5).

Day 15

"We've had bad luck with our kids—
they've all grown up."
—Christopher Morley

had a student in an English class I was once teaching tell me the most beautiful story. I was talking to them about my life growing up as a biracial child. For me, the combining of two different cultures has been precious. I never had any real confusion about who I was or where I belonged, though I have heard stories from other biracial children who did need some sense of clarity. I think for me, the difference is that I grew up with both my Black father and White mother who loved each other dearly. There was really not much room for confusion then, because I knew them both, loved them both, and knew that they loved me. I never worried about fitting in, because I didn't really ever have unresolved questions about one side of my heritage. They were both there, and both were supportive.

A student in my class then told me a story about her son. He had been attending his first year of school and often came home raving to his mother about his new friend. When she tucked him in at night, he told her all the fun stories from his school day playing with his comrade. In the morning when he got up, he was excited to go back to school because he knew his friend was going to be there. One day she came in earlier than usual to pick up her son. He saw her at the door and came running, as children often do when they catch a glimpse of Mom. He gave her a hug and then immediately pointed across the room so that he could show her who his new friend was.

"He's right there!" he said, beaming and pointing.

"Which one?" she asked, perplexed as she followed his tiny finger into a sea of children.

"The kid in the red shirt!" he said excitedly.

When her eyes landed on her child's friend, she couldn't help smiling. In a class with 25 or so little children running around, every child in her son's room was White, except the dark skin of her son's best friend, who was wearing a red shirt. In a room where everyone shared the same skin tone but one, her son could not think of one single characteristic that would identify his friend to his mother from the other children in the room, except for his red shirt.

When she told me that story, I was moved. There is a reason that Christ said that in order to enter the kingdom of heaven, we would first need to become like children. Children are precious. Children don't hate until they are first taught hate.

There are a lot of things Jesus could use to point us out to His Father. I can just see Him discussing bringing me into the kingdom.

"That's her!" He'd say, beaming as He pointed me out to God the Father.

"Which one?" He'd respond. Now at this point there are a million things Jesus could use to identify me. He could point me out as the girl that's been a hypocrite or the same girl who stole that ankle bracelet from the convenience store in ninth grade and to this day has never been caught for it. The girl who threw up all over her twin bed the first time she got drunk in high school or that girl who lost her cool and spewed a few choice words when she got cut off on the highway, and that one was more recent than I'd like to admit.

We try not to tell each other about our shortcomings, because we fear we will lose respect then. We keep things from one another, sometimes even from our closest friends, for fear that if they found out they wouldn't see us anymore, but they'd see the sin. I read a devotional entry once by Max Lucado in his book *Just Like Jesus,* in which he talked about a personal friend who had an affair. The affair had happened more than 10 years ago, and the husband, never confessed it. When his wife finally did find out 10 years later, they dropped everything and took a trip together to put out the noise of the world and focus on each other and their relationship.

As I read this part, I did what I often do while reading or listening to stories: I put myself in the leading character's shoes. I thought, *If that were my husband, I would leave him.* I am not saying that is the right thing to do, and I am not saying that is what everyone else should do. I am simply saying what I *think* I would do in this situation. I've had this discussion with my husband as well. I let him know when we were dating that if he ever cheated on me, that would be it. In past relationships I have tolerated a lot of inappropriate behavior, but cheating, luckily, was never one of them.

I have heard it argued in some research studies that a man can physically cheat and his love, or love in the marriage, not be gone. That a man can make this mistake and still love his wife, recognize the mistake, and move forward.

With women, this is far less typical. If a woman cheats physically, it was already over for her emotionally. By the time you find out she cheated, she probably is already leaving you. It is rare for a woman to impulse on something physical without already experiencing emotional detachment.

When talking about emotions and jealousy with my students, I share with them that research shows that women experience the most jealousy if they feel their partner is experiencing emotional attachment to someone else. Men, on the other hand, experience the most jealousy if they fear their partner is experiencing physical attachments with someone else. I typically ask my students if they agree with this, and every time, most of the males say they would be angrier about physical cheating, and the females say they would be angrier about emotional cheating. I would be equally as angry about either one.

In Max Lucado's book the couple is on vacation together, reflecting and crying, and trying to figure out where they go from here. The woman is trying to figure out if she can move on from this infidelity. Lucado says this: "In this case the wife was clearly in the right. She could have left. Women have done so for lesser reasons. Or she could have stayed and made his life a living hell. Other women have done that. But she chose a different response.

"On the tenth night of their trip my friend found a card on his pillow. On the card was a printed verse: 'I'd rather do nothing with you than something without you.' Beneath the verse she had written these words: *I forgive you. I love you. Let's move on.*"

I was struck by this story, because in the character of this woman, I recognized the character of Christ. Romans 3:23 reminds us, "For all have sinned and fall short of the glory of God."

We do not deserve Christ. We have hurt Him, we have disgraced Him, we have betrayed Him, and if He came back right now, I believe many of us would crucify Him all over again. If you are sunk in the guilt of your past, so much so that you cannot breathe or move, lie still, because Jesus wants you. In fact, He would rather lie there doing nothing with you than something without you. On your pillow is a card, and on that card is a note penned from the hand of Christ that reads, "*I forgive you. I love you. Let's move on.*"

Jesus Christ is so good, because everything we have done, every secret sin He's seen us do in the dark, means nothing to Him the second we have sincerely repented and sought His forgiveness. I'm not perfect, but at least I know what a loser I am; and because of that, I am forced to seek His shelter and guidance every morning the second my eyelids open. Yes, there are a million different things Jesus could use to point me out to the Father. Lucky for me, He'll just stand there beaming, proud to point me out in the crowd. And the single characteristic that He notices that would distinguish loser me from a roomful of saints is my red shirt.

In heaven we'll all be wearing red. It will be the color for every season. Trust me, no matter what you've done or where you've been, you can still seek the refuge of Christ, and when you do, stand tall and proud to slip on that beautiful, distinguishable, bright-red shirt.

"That's My friend!" Jesus will say, smiling. "The one washed in the blood of the Lamb."

Reflection: "And he said: 'Truly I tell you, unless you change and become like little children, you will never enter the kingdom of heaven'" (Matthew 18:3).

Day 16

"You can know the name of a bird in all the languages of the world, but when you're finished, you'll know absolutely nothing whatever about the bird. . . . So let's look at the bird and see what it's doing—that's what counts. I learned very early the difference between knowing the name of something and knowing something."

—Richard Feynman

One of the things that always stands out to me while reading through the Bible is not the lack of faith by the people of ancient times, but more so the overabundance of faith. There were gods for everything, and idols and worship were not only sacred; they were everywhere. Every great king believed in the power of a great god, and every soldier prayed to a being that they believed would protect them in times of battle. Religion was not a thing for fools; it was a way of life. This is so contrary to the way our world is now. God finally got the point through to people—that worshipping objects that could be made by the hands of people was not reliable, and so what do we go and do? Instead of acknowledging Jesus as Lord, we now fight the battle of acknowledging any maker at all.

I think one of the main problems with faith is that we think we have to rely on faith without knowledge. I have recently been reading a book that a professor recommended to me called *Knowing Christ Today*, by Dallas Willard. In it he summarizes that if there were any other aspect of life that we did not know to be true on the basis of fact alone, and yet believed anyway, we would be crazy. Willard says that a problem with faith is that we assume we have to jump into it without knowledge. You aren't a good Christian if you don't just "believe" that God is real without doing any other search for facts. The problem that comes from this, then, is how do we as Christians take our newfound faith to others without first knowing why we believe what we believe? Willard says that knowledge improves faith, and on this point I agree with him.

That being said, I also believe that blind faith has power. When Jesus was resurrected and went to meet the disciples, Thomas said that until he felt the scars with his own hands he would not believe. In John 20:27-29 Jesus appears to Thomas and says, 'Put your finger here; see my hands.

Reach out your hand and put it into my side. Stop doubting and believe.' Thomas said to him, 'My Lord and my God!' Then Jesus told him, 'Because you have seen me, you have believed; blessed are those who have not seen and yet have believed.'"

You see, I understand that faith has value, but I also believe that we can add to our faith by experiencing and seeking knowledge. While teaching communications at a secular college, I have had the experience, while watching and listening as young people come and go from their classrooms, that if a Christian wishes to attend a non-Christian college, it is important that their faith be rock-solid. Unfortunately, that is a lot to ask. The average Christian doesn't study or research why others don't believe God exists; they are simply taught that He does and not to question it.

Regrettably, they are then thrown into classrooms, where they meet charismatic, highly intelligent, and very successful professors who will counter their belief in God, and not just with opinions, but also with much research that they will present as proof. Religion in a secular school is taught as a philosophy. It is not scientific, and, therefore, is simply thrown in there with all the other philosophical ideas people may choose to embrace, such as Greek mythology, Hinduism, and Buddhism (which by the way, tend to be viewed more positively than Christianity). When a Christ-believing, churchgoing student finds an objection in their professor's lecture and tries to voice their concern, they often find that faith doesn't get you very far when you're arguing against someone with credible research and knowledge that suddenly seems so much bigger than your "feelings." And, in my opinion, this is another reason that 60 percent of young people are leaving our church: Because they don't research why they believe what they believe, and when they meet someone who has, it can tarnish their faith.

Fact: Jesus existed. We have historical documents proving this, so this issue is not up for discussion. In fact, I remember reading about Jesus in my public high school history book. The majority of scholars agree that a man named Jesus lived, though there are a few who deny that He ever existed at all. (But there will always be conspiracy theorists.) The idea that Jesus lived and was a leader with followers is not up for debate, even in most Darwinian rhetoric. The issue is not is Jesus a real person, but rather was He who He said He was, and how can we be sure?

David Williams, a computer systems manager for the mathematics faculty at the University of New Castle, said this when discussing the Bible's prophecy: "For example, what's the likelihood of a person predicting today the exact city in which the birth of a future leader would take place, well into the twenty-first century? This is indeed what the prophet Micah did 700 years before the Messiah. Further, what is the likelihood of predicting the precise manner of death that a new, unknown religious leader would experience, a thousand years from now—a manner of death presently unknown, and to remain unknown for hundreds of years? Yet this is what David did in 1000 B.C. Again, what is the likelihood of predicting the specific date of the appearance of some great future leader, hundreds of years in advance? This is what Daniel did, 530 years before Christ."

Peter Stoner, a professor and mathematician, discusses biblical prophecy in his book *Science Speaks*. In this book he examines the best proof, or access to knowledge, that we as Christians have regarding Christ as the Messiah. The Bible was not just a tool given to us to better understand morality; it is also a prophetic and holy message that proves that Christ is who He said He is. The more people that understand biblical prophecy and use this understanding as a base for their faith, the better people will be able to explain to nonbelievers why they believe so wholeheartedly.

Stoner did a study using one of his classes and found that there were more than 300 prophecies concerning Jesus as the Messiah in Old Testament Scripture. When Jesus was on this earth, He lived 33 years, and in that time fulfilled all 300 of these prophecies. Stoner found that the probability of one person fulfilling just eight of the prophecies was calculated at one chance in 10^{17} (one followed by 17 zeros). I feel as though this number has to be written out in order to see its massiveness. Stoner discovers that someone fulfilling just eight of the 300 prophecies is calculated at one chance in 100,000,000,000,000,000. I'm no math person, but that is one big number. It would be impossible for one person to arrange the city of their birth before their birth, or arrange their death to fit a certain style of torture and murder, or to arrange to have their murderers gamble for their shoes, though Scripture tells us that with Christ this is exactly what took place.

To make a picture of what all this math looks like, Stoner says that you would have to take the state of Texas and fill it two feet deep with silver dollars. Before I go on, I should also explain to you just how big the state of Texas is. To get a mass the size of Texas, you would have to combine Ohio, Indiana, and the Middle Atlantic states. Once these are all combined, you have a place the size of Texas. So once all 268,581 square miles (695,622 square kilometers) of Texas are covered two feet deep in silver dollars, you would need to put a giant X on one of the silver dollars and then toss it back somewhere in Texas. Next is the fun part: You blindfold a man, or a woman, or a child, or even a monkey, and send them into Texas. Then they bend down and reach their hand into the 268,581-square-mile area of Texas and, on their first try, pick up the one silver dollar with the big X on it. This is what one in 10^{17} looks like. Stoner found that, mathematically speaking, based on probability and concepts, the likelihood of this happening is the same as Jesus Christ fulfilling just eight of the 300 prophecies He fulfilled. That silver dollar is comparable to eight prophecies, and Jesus fulfilled 300. There is not a number big enough to even contain what Christ did.

Stoner concludes, "Any man who rejects Christ as the Son of God is rejecting a fact, proved perhaps more absolutely than any other fact in the world" (Stoner, p. 112).

We should not be afraid of knowledge. God is knowledge. We believe in Christ as the Messiah because God proved it to us by systematically evidencing it, so much so that our greatest mathematicians cannot even calculate His work. We must share our knowledge of Christ as the Messiah with others. I don't just have faith that Jesus is Christ, I know that Jesus is Christ, because the Bible tells me so.

Reflection: "No one lights a lamp and puts it in a place where it will be hidden, or under a bowl. Instead they put it on its stand, so that those who come in may see the light" (Luke 11:33).

Day 17

"I am not afraid of an army of lions led by a sheep;
I am afraid of an army of sheep led by a lion."

—Alexander the Great

My husband and I went for a jog yesterday evening. It's the beginning of August, and with the threat of summer slipping through our fingers, we had no choice but to head outside and enjoy the cool breeze of dusk. I am also six months pregnant, and wanting to at least attempt to keep some of my previous figure. At the end of our run and during our cooldown walk, my husband waved at a car that passed. It was a teacher he had had in high school, and she was on her way home from visiting her son. She pulled into our driveway, and we chatted for a few moments. She asked how my husband was doing.

"Good," he said.

"I mean spiritually. How are you doing spiritually?" This particular woman was also in charge of the Sabbath school at my husband's home church. She often asked Seth this question when she saw him, and it always made me smile. Seth is blessed with a great talent of public speaking, and though he is terribly shy in normal conversation, while at a pulpit he is able to transform into a tool in the hand of Christ. I love watching him speak, because I know it is a gift from God since it is completely contradictory to his personality.

I also know that he is humble. Where many may get confused by the accolades after a well-spoken sermon, Seth is genuinely moved to tears because he knows that Christ was just with him. When I speak, I don't think I am all that special because it is not a surprise that someone who likes talking, works as a professor, and is in love with words would also enjoy public speaking. This is all a part of my personality and is to be expected.

My husband, on the other hand, is completely my opposite. I tell him that he is probably every teacher's worst nightmare because he is that student that a teacher calls on to share their thoughts and looks at them sheepishly as if he has nothing to say. Put him in a small group, big group, one on one, or playing games (all the methods we teachers use to engage these shy, back-of-the-classroom students), and he is still not talking. Seth hates attention. He likes to listen and watch people way more than he likes talking.

It is because of him that I seek out my shy students every semester. I hunt them down, because I know that just because they are shy does not mean they are not paying attention. Quiet people often have the greatest insights because they've been listening and watching intently. People like myself, with their hands raised first, may also have insight, but they probably didn't spend too much time thinking about the question. We just like to talk. Typically, when my husband says something, it isn't just to talk; it is because he actually has something to say. This is a quality I do not possess, although I admire it.

Even when he prepares to lead in Bible study, he spends an entire week in deep prayer and meditation, accompanied by Scripture reading. I read up a bit the day before, run it through in my mind, and then jot down some notes before sharing what I learned. This works for me, but my husband would never do it this way and looks at me horrified as I prepare. You see, I talk in front of about 100 students every semester, and so I don't panic about it; and while I also pray and ask God to prepare my heart and my tongue, I also can rely on the gifts that He has already given me. My husband relies 98 percent on Christ and 2 percent on his previous knowledge and experiences. I suppose this is why he is the one studying to be a pastor, and I am not. A fact I am OK with. He is incredibly opposite to me, and Christ will find a way to use us both, playing to our different strengths.

I loved that this woman hadn't seen my husband in months and yet felt comfortable enough to ask him how he was doing spiritually. She didn't say it condescendingly or proudly; she was sincerely asking, and I thought it was beautiful. That is what Christian brotherhood looks like, holding one another accountable not out of judgment but love and sincerity.

"I'm getting to where I should be, just slowly," he said in response to her question.

"Well, remember the story I told you about what the shepherd does to the naughty sheep?" she asked. She proceeded to explain a practice in the Middle East that shepherds use on their sheep that often wander away from the fold. Often if one sheep wanders, others may follow, and it causes confusion for the other sheep as to which way to go. Do they follow the shepherd or their fellow sheep? To thwart this from happening, the shepherd will often break the leg of his rebellious sheep and carry it on his shoulders till the sheep's leg heals. The shepherd does not want to lose one sheep, not to mention all the sheep that may have followed the rebellious one. So instead of getting rid of the wayward sheep, he will first break its leg to teach it the importance of following the shepherd and hope that this will teach the sheep not to wander.

"God would rather break your leg than let you wander off," she said. "Learn from my mistakes, and don't be so stubborn that He has no other choice." She smiled, asked about the baby, and then went home.

Sometimes we are too independent to remember that Christ is the shepherd and we are nothing but sheep. He has a destination for you. He has the map, knows where you should be going, and is even willing to take you there Himself. Sometimes, though, our hearts will wander. We see rocks or hills and lose sight of the fact that He is the one with the map. We think we know a better way, a shorter way, an easier way, or we are just too tired to go anywhere at all.

Find rest at the feet of the Shepherd. Perhaps right now you've found your legs are broken. It's OK, because He isn't expecting that now you will have to walk this journey on broken legs more tired and painful than would have previously been your course. On the contrary, He is ready to carry you on His very own shoulders, anything to ensure that His precious little sheep makes its way home.

Reflection: "Know that the Lord is God. It is he who made us, and we are his; we are his people, the sheep of his pasture" (Psalm 100:3).

Day 18

"Your religion is what you do
when the sermon is over."

—*P.S. I Love You*, compiled by H. Jackson Brown, Jr.

I was born into a Seventh-day Adventist family. I'm not sure how much I enjoyed the Sabbath as a child. Often I just waited for the minutes to tick away so it could be sundown. My parents took a "Sabbath nap," and this is probably what started my lack of appreciation for the seventh day of the week. I didn't mind church. I liked to learn about Jesus, and I liked seeing my friends. Sabbath lunch was always a plus. My family usually sat down to eat our dinners together all week, but Sabbath lunch was always the best food; and though I hated waiting till 2:00 to have lunch, it was usually worth it. Thanks for that, Mom! Typically the problem kicked in after lunch. My parents would maybe take us on a walk if it was summer, but I could be assured that sometime shortly after, they would take their nap and I would be forced against my will to either sleep with them or stay awake staring at a wall in protest.

The older I got, the more I grew to appreciate my Sabbath. I started working, and it became the sanctuary I needed it to be. I've worked hard my whole life. That was one principle my parents made clear to my sister and me. We were going to work and make our own money. Our first Nintendo was purchased in third grade from our own funds. Our trampoline we got the summer after was also bought with our own money.

It honestly has only been in the past year that I have not worked on a Sunday. My senior year in high school I sent my tiny résumé out to all the local radio stations, because at this point I still wanted to be a journalist. I got hired at 17 years old at a station in Benton Harbor, Michigan, and started out as a reporter interviewing senators, congressmen, and state representatives (it was an election year). Eventually, I got my own weekend radio show that I did on Sundays, and so I worked six days out of seven, and grew to really appreciate the rest and family time that Sabbath brought to my week.

After I graduated high school, I started partying for a brief time period in my life. It really wasn't that long, but as I have said before, whatever I do, I do till I'm the best at it. If I am a student, I am going to be the best student; if I am writing a book, I am going to give it all my attention until I feel that I have put together the best book I could have; and so since I was partying, I was going to party like I was the wildest, craziest, most fun girl at the party. My weekend started on Thursday after classes, and I partied till Saturday morning, at which point I would pause to sit in my church pew. Out of respect, I'd typically wait till sundown Saturday, and then resume my partying till I had to be to work on Sunday morning.

As I reflect on all that now, I find it ironic how I felt like such a faithful Adventist when I turned down a promotion my boss offered me at the radio station because it would mean I had to work on Sabbath. "I just can't do it. It's my Sabbath," I told him, completely ignoring the fact that I had just partied like a rock star the previous Friday evening. Sometimes I have to marvel at my own hypocrisy.

One day, however, I was doing my daily Bible read and stumbled upon Isaiah 56:2, which says, "Blessed is the one who does this—the person who holds it fast, who keeps the Sabbath without desecrating it, and keeps their hands from doing any evil."

The verse really spoke to me. God sent Isaiah to speak to Israel at a time when they were worshipping other gods, sacrificing their children to these false gods, and intermarrying with other religions, and yet amidst all this perversion, God gives Isaiah a message about the Sabbath.

Isaiah goes on to explain in verses 6 and 7, "All who keep the Sabbath without desecrating it and who hold fast to my covenant—these I will bring to my holy mountain and give them joy in my house of prayer. Their burnt offerings and sacrifices will be accepted on my altar; for my house will be called a house of prayer for all nations."

This message spoke to me because I was desecrating His Sabbath. I started searching the Bible then for other Sabbath-related verses, and I knew that I had offended God, and that was something that I didn't want to do, because I did love Him.

I didn't quit drinking immediately, but I did quit drinking on the Sabbath. I can remember my brother making fun of me. "So it is OK to drink the other days of the week as long as you don't drink on Sabbath?" he'd say. I understood what he was saying and I still do, but I hadn't been convicted on alcohol yet; what I had been convicted of was the fact that the

Sabbath was holy and that I was desecrating that holiness by mingling it with irreverence.

Unlike people, God appreciates all our efforts, even when they come in the form of baby steps. For another project I am currently working on, I will often try to think of characteristics that I know God possesses and then how I have seen Him display those characteristics in our relationship. I think it is important to remember that God is real. He is a real person, and this relationship is real. It changes the way I talk with Him, pray with Him, and read with Him.

Even this morning when I started my prayer, I started by saying, "Lord, thank You for waking me up this morning, thank You for my family, protect us, be with me today . . . ," and I had to stop myself. I cannot pray to God out of routine and habit—humming songs already sung. I had to rewind, remind myself that this is a real conversation, that He is right there, listening; and I think He appreciates me pausing, thinking, and then talking to Him as though I actually believe He is interested in what I have to say that day.

I had to pause myself and remember that there is a vast difference between saying prayers and praying. Martin Luther, a scholar who questioned some of the Catholic Church's practices in the late 1400s and early 1500s, once said, "The fewer the words, the better the prayer."

There is certainly something powerful about meditation. I don't mean the idea of meditation we see in these counterfeit Eastern religions. I don't mean yoga, or Zen, where the goal is to empty the mind. I mean the meditation that requires you to fill the mind. The only thing God wants you to empty your mind of is the garbage you may have been putting into it. When it comes to the Word, or inspired readings, He wants you to fill your mind.

One of the characteristics I truly love about God is that He deals with us individually. Because of this, I shouldn't ever try to understand why He is working in a certain way in the life of someone else that I know He would never do with me. God knows the hearts of His children, and because of that, where I may look at someone, or my brother may have looked at me, and thought, *You fool!* I think God saw that my motives were sincere and genuine. He sees me as an individual, and thank goodness He isn't comparing me to anyone else.

Drinking may be foolish, but allowing yourself to play a fool on a day that God proclaimed holy was smacking Christ as the Creator in the face.

I felt that it compared to showing up drunk at your wedding ceremony or on your father's birthday. It was disrespecting the person by disrespecting the event, and maybe I didn't have enough respect for myself at that point in my life to quit drinking, but I did respect God enough not to disrespect His event.

I bring this up in this devotional because I don't think I am some Adventist rogue. I know there are others, a lot like I was, who do respect Christ and just haven't made that full commitment to Him yet. The beautiful thing about our Lord is that He is proud of baby steps. I am not going to ask you to stop drinking today if that is something you struggle with, though tomorrow I will talk about what led me to quit. What I do have to ask you is that you respect God and His Sabbath. The Sabbath is holy, and I think because we are Adventists and have been Adventist, we are so immersed in the Adventist culture that we forget the whole reason behind the Sabbath. The Sabbath is the seal between creation and Creator. It is a day of reflection that is marked by His holy hands. It is precious to Christ, and, therefore, should be respected by us.

Satan loves every second that he gets us to disregard something he knows Christ holds dear. He lives for those moments, because then he can laugh because God gave His life for a people who continually reject everything He stands for. I think we first have to recognize just how awesome God is. Don't allow yourself or your life to be a tool used by the evil one to diminish the life and work of Christ. I know you love God; you wouldn't be reading this book if you weren't concerned about your relationship with Him. Loving God is easy; it's learning to respect Him that will force you to reevaluate the way you're treating Him. God deserves respect, and, luckily, that it is one gift you can freely give.

Reflection: "Remember the Sabbath day by keeping it holy" (Exodus 20:8).

Day 19

A man consulted a doctor. "I've been misbehaving, Doc, and my conscience is troubling me," he complained.

"And you want something that will strengthen your willpower?" asked the doctor.

"Well, no," said the fellow. "I was thinking of something that would weaken my conscience."

If I were being honest about my life, I would have to tell you that I didn't quit drinking for myself. I've never been addicted to alcohol, and so even after I quit partying and realized that belligerence was anything but becoming of a woman, I did not stop drinking altogether. I believed that drinking in moderation was completely acceptable, though I knew that it wasn't healthy. I didn't really see that much harm in one glass of wine with a girlfriend. I know this is an issue that affects a lot of young Adventists, or just Protestant Christians in general. I decided pretty quickly after a partying stint I had been on that getting drunk just wasn't for me.

For one thing, I didn't have the stomach for it, and I simply decided that not remembering the things I said and did the day before was not my idea of a good time. I like my life and the moments in it to mean something. I realized that the bonds with friends I was creating over drunken nights were really displaying a lack of genuine friendship. To prove this point, I can tell you that literally 95 percent of the friends who used to be my absolute best friends in the world don't even talk to me anymore since I have quit drinking. We just don't have enough in common, which proves to me that we probably never did, and that alcohol allows for a lack of genuine substance in relationships. I also realized that not having control over myself was not fun or attractive. It's funny, because every girl who sees another girl completely wasted looks at that girl as if she were trash, all the while ignoring the fact that they have indeed been that girl many times over.

So I quit partying and drinking excessively because I realized that biblically it was wrong, and just personally I didn't like portraying myself as a woman in that light. I finally started getting some self-respect, and I think a lot of that came from the friend in Christ I was making. Though I was not doing any bar crawls, I was still drinking casually from time to time with a few girlfriends. To be honest, though, even while drinking moderately, I still felt sort of disconnected from God because of the alcohol. I blamed that on my Adventist upbringing, because when I read the Bible for myself, I couldn't really find any verses telling me that alcohol in moderation was a sin. I found that alcohol was foolish and that it would lead to sin, but no direct condemnation of one glass of wine. Really, I was grasping at straws to find excuses for my own behavior.

I decided to stop drinking when I read the books by the apostle Paul. I learned a lot from him while reading Scripture. Essentially, Paul says that he chooses not to do certain things (in my case, drink), not because of himself, but because he does not want to be a stumbling block for the person sitting next to him.

This resonated deeply with me. You see, I was no alcoholic, and had decided that drinking to excess was not something that I enjoyed. I did not fear that my drinking moderately was going to keep me out of heaven. I should note, though, that I have since realized that God never wants you to indulge in sin, even in moderation.

Something just seems to happen, though, the more you get to know God. You start to truly develop feelings for His people, and that is what happened to me. I didn't want someone who did have a drinking problem or could have a drinking problem to start struggling because seeing me drinking allowed them to excuse their own habits. I know that this happens, because I have seen it in my own life. We as people feel strength in numbers, and so if a lot of people are doing something that we think may be wrong, we decide it can't be that bad. I want to be strong where someone else may be weak if it will help them in their walk with Christ. In fact, I think we don't fully realize just how much Christ is going to hold us accountable for the things we did that caused others to sin. That sin will be on your hands.

This reasoning by Paul made complete sense to me, and so I had to change my own behaviors because as Christians, we are witnesses not only to those who do not know God, but also to those who know Him and are struggling, just as we are. The thing about alcohol is that it really can be a vicious snare in someone's life. I have a dear friend who says that she'd rather her father be a bank robber than an alcoholic because she has watched alcohol completely destroy their lives. In fact, she has said she would rather him be a heroin user, meth abuser, or cokehead than be an alcoholic, because of the social acceptance alcohol has. A drug addict feels separated from society because of their addiction, whereas alcoholics often don't recognize there is a problem until it is too late. Not to mention that no one seems to take alcoholics seriously because it is so socially acceptable. An alcoholic tries to tell their friends they are not drinking that night because they want to slow down, and their friends tell them that they're being dramatic. Because alcohol is socially acceptable, it can be the worst drug to be addicted to.

I will also note here that, so far, all my reasoning for not drinking is mostly geared toward women. That is only because I am a woman and I explain things from my perspective, but alcohol, in my opinion, is just as vicious in men. Men drink and get angry. They almost can't help it. It's like it is a spike to their alpha-male inside and somehow triggers their anger button. Research shows men tend to express anger more readily than women. For men, anger is a default emotion. Someone hurts them, but they don't want to show sadness because that makes them look weak, and so they show anger. Jealousy becomes anger, sorrow becomes anger, pain becomes anger, and alcohol heightens those feelings of anger.

Women drink and look trashy, or worse, put themselves in sexual situations they never would have if they had been sober. Getting drunk and getting taken advantage of is not my idea of a party; it is sad. Men drink and get violent toward women or other men, or put their fists through walls because they are mad at themselves. Not to even mention that alcohol is a downer and causes depression.

What I love about Paul is that he leaves us no straws to grasp. OK, so alcohol doesn't affect you like that. Well, odds are, it does affect the people on your right and left like that, and you are a stumbling block to those people just by joining them. I can assure you that you will one day be held accountable for everything you did to yourself and everything you caused someone else to do.

Before I close, I want to address one issue someone could be thinking. *How can my actions lead someone else to sin? Isn't each person accountable for the things they do?* Yes and no. We are all accountable for our own actions; we are even accountable for the actions we commit that lead someone else to stumble. For example, Satan didn't make Eve sin; he subtly led her to sin, and in return, she didn't make Adam sin, but by her actions she caused him to. Jezebel didn't make Ahab sin, but as every woman knows, women have a great power of suggestion to their men, and she used this to cause Ahab to sin greatly against God. All these people were punished not just for their own sin, but the sin they lured someone else to commit.

Ellen White says in *Prophets and Kings*, "We lead others either upward to happiness and immortal life, or downward to sorrow and eternal death. And if by our deeds we strengthen or force into activity the evil powers of those around us, we share their sin" (p. 94).

Theologian Tryon Edwards once said, "Whoever in prayer can say, 'Our Father,' acknowledges and should feel the brotherhood of the whole race of mankind." God's will is that we will become one with each other. The only way this thing called Christianity can really take flight is if we don't just start caring about our walk with Christ, but we also start caring about how we can influence someone else's. The generation before us had a move toward individuality and separateness. There was this push in American culture that what I do affects only me, and if you don't like it, tough. A characteristic of this mediavore, millennial generation, is that we strive for community. We strive for brotherhood. We want group-orientated learning and acceptance.

I like to remember and really allow the quotes of famous authors and writers to sink in and marinate my mind. If you haven't noticed, I enjoy words, and even more so, well-crafted words by people who made their words matter. That being said, I have one more quote for you today. Jesus, Son of David, Jesus of Nazareth, Jesus, the one whom they called Christ, once said in Luke 10:27, "'Love the Lord your God with all your heart and with all your soul and with all your strength and with all your mind'; and 'Love your neighbor as yourself.'" Love your neighbor. Love your sister, love your brother, love your church family, your gas station attendant, your nurse, your waiter, your taxi driver, your lifeguard, your teacher, your classmate, and even the neighbor whose name you haven't taken the time yet to know—love them as yourself. This is a powerful statement.

I am currently in a Bible study with a friend who has taken on the position that alcohol in moderation is biblically acceptable. I cannot get too angry at him for this, because I used to say the same thing, though ignorantly. What I have come to realize is this: Do I really believe that God would be OK with me practicing foolishness, as long as I do it in moderation? Of course not! Proverbs 20:1 says, "Wine is a mocker and beer a brawler; whoever is led astray by them is not wise."

God does not lead His children into foolishness and evil, but rather delivers them from evil. In Psalm 75:8 we see that God's anger is compared to mixed wine drank by the wicked. "In the hand of the Lord is a cup full of foaming wine mixed with spices; he pours it out, and all the wicked of the earth drink it down to its very dregs."

Alcohol is foolish, and Christ doesn't need a generation that practices foolishness in moderation. He needs a church that will stand and reflect His image fully. This is a time-sensitive message, because, you see, you are not just any church or any people at any time in history. I believe we are the last church, the final generation, and this is the end of days. How do you spiritually feed a generation who is already stuffed full with the media's perception of right and wrong, and in which drinking is not only acceptable but popular? You remind them of the words of Joshua in 24:15. You can serve the media, serve the world and follow their idols. You can find your peace through Yoga and Zen. You can do that. He has allowed you that freedom. But a choice, one way or the other, has to be made. Choose today whom you will serve, them or Him? As for me and my house, we will serve the Lord.

Christ did not die just for you; He died for you and the person sitting next to you. Do not allow a life, which Christ died for, to be lost because of your weakened conscience, but instead strengthen your willpower. Sometimes the closest to God someone else is going to get is you.

Reflection: "Let us therefore make every effort to do what leads to peace and to mutual edification. Do not destroy the work of God for the sake of food. All food is clean, but it is wrong for a person to eat anything that causes someone else to stumble. It is better not to eat meat or drink wine or to do anything else that will cause your brother or sister to fall" (Romans 14:19-21).

Day 20

"All say, 'How hard it is that we have to die'—a strange complaint to come from the mouths of people who have had to live."
—Mark Twain

My uncle died yesterday. It was humbling and enlightening to be able to be with him in his last few hours of life. Since his passing I have been left feeling a sort of emptiness. The older I get, and the more time with God I spend, the more I realize that this world is futile. I told my husband that I can't help feeling slightly disconnected from life when I realize how fragile and pointless it all is. The words of Solomon resonate with me deeply right now as death leaves this world seeming rather meaningless. I sat in a room with my family singing hymns as my uncle Larry got the courage to let his body fall asleep. I watched my mother hold the hand of her big brother and sob as his pulse faded. I heard the cries of my grandparents, who have now lost their second son, and in contrast, I felt the kicks of life from my daughter in my womb.

In the same room I marveled as one man lost connection to this world, all the while a little girl was growing and asserting herself to be able to enter it. It was sobering to me, and I couldn't help entering my own state of rigor mortis as my mind pummeled me with deep feelings of insignificance. The great paradox in this world is that every great life will be marked with death, and yet we are a people who cleave to a notion of immortality. We think death is for everyone else, and we live that way till our time ticks out.

In the aftermath of my thoughts I am left with one conclusion. If I can teach my daughter only one important lesson about this life, I hope it is this: The only thing that matters in this world is that you live your life to bring glory to God. One day we will all be on a bed in a small room with not much left but a tiny tank of air in our lungs. And in that moment it is not going to matter that you are pretty, or smart, or rich, or thin, or powerful. Trust me: your success will turn frail in the face of death. If you are not living each day to meet Christ's objective for your life, then not only will you shortly cease to exist, but you really never should have existed at all. This world is simply the entrance exam to heaven, and if you do not pass, you don't just fail and get to try something else; you are out of the game.

No one likes the fire-and-brimstone approach to life, but suddenly my heart is struck with the notion that whatever it takes to get the message through is exactly the route that should be traveled. We cannot live for ourselves and expect to die in Christ. Live for Christ, die in Christ, and awake in Christ. This is Day 20 in our journey together, and I pray sincerely that you will stop and take a few moments right here to really put your relationship with God at the forefront of everything else. I know the Redeemer lives because yesterday, even amidst death, I felt life and was moved. The Bible tells us in Isaiah 57:1, 2, "The devout are taken away, and no one understands that the righteous are taken away to be spared from evil. Those who walk uprightly enter into peace; they find rest as they lie in death." Through Christ there is peace in death because the race is over and you have won. Yes, this life is simply an entrance exam, and once your timer stops, it won't matter what you could have done, should have done, or would have done. All that will matter is what you did and how you did it.

In contrast to our previous passage, verses 20, 21 say, "But the wicked are like the tossing sea, which cannot rest, whose waves cast up mire and mud. 'There is no peace,' says my God, 'for the wicked.'"

I am reminded as I ponder these verses of our discussion on Day 1. This life is short. It is but a moment, and Satan is hoping that you will live your whole life feeling immortal until the second that it is suddenly stripped from you. It all goes back to the very first lie he told Eve in the garden, "You will not surely die." If we believe that time is stationary and that we can always get more of it, then why not live for ourselves until we absolutely have to make the switch?

It is only now that I understand why some Christians are against these vampire books that pose immortality to our children. It is easy to get caught up in the fantasy that you will not surely die. There is a reason this is the first lie the devil tells. He is not a second-rate opponent. This is someone who calculates his every move. He wants us to forget that every one of us will die, because something happens when we recognize just how futile this life is, that it is only here for a moment and that it will not last and is not meant to. When we recognize that, we start to make it matter. We seek to make things right with the Creator when death is imminent. There is a reason there are no atheists in the foxhole. Satan wants you to read stories of beings that will not die, cannot die, where immortality is prevalent and death is not a factor. Distraction can be fatal.

One of my favorite Bible texts deals with God's everlasting mercy.

In Luke 23 we see the story of Christ's crucifixion as relayed by Luke. In verses 32-38 we see the last few hours as Jesus is living through them: "Two other men, both criminals, were also led out with him to be executed. When they came to the place called the Skull, they crucified him there, along with the criminals—one on his right, the other on his left. Jesus said, 'Father, forgive them, for they do not know what they are doing.' And they divided up his clothes by casting lots. The people stood watching, and the rulers even sneered at him. They said, 'He saved others; let him save himself if he is God's Messiah, the Chosen One.' The soldiers also came up and mocked him. They offered him wine vinegar and said, 'If you are the king of the Jews, save yourself.' There was a written notice above him, which read: This is the King of the Jews."

And then we see a scene displayed that proves the thoughts fallacious of those who try to exclaim that God is a bloodthirsty tyrant. These words are from the mouths of people who have just enough knowledge of Scripture to be dangerous, but are clearly out of their depth. Jesus, the one whom they called Christ, does something incredible. In the midst of His own misery, in the midst of snide remarks, bodily exhaustion, and severe agony, He puts aside the self and provides redemption for the broken.

Verses 39-43 record, "One of the criminals who hung there hurled insults at him: 'Aren't you the Messiah? Save yourself and us!' But the other criminal rebuked him. 'Don't you fear God,' he said, 'since you are under the same sentence? We are punished justly, for we are getting what our deeds deserve. But this man has done nothing wrong.' Then he said, 'Jesus, remember me when you come into your kingdom.' Jesus answered him, 'Truly I tell you today, you will be with me in paradise.'"

The mercy of God is that even on one's deathbed after a life of shutting up that still small voice, He hears the cries of the sincere. He hung on the cross between two thieves at His crucifixion, and to one of them He promised eternal life. It is never too late to meet Jesus, but it can be too late to live a life that matters.

Six months ago doctors gave my uncle six months to live. In His mercy, Christ gave my uncle six months to prepare his heart and mind for death and eternal life. Unfortunately, we do not all get six months. For some of us, we will have a mere moment.

It is by no coincidence that in these last days, Satan would rather have you focusing on vampires, wizards, and immortality. In the real world there is birth and death, evil and good. In the real world we have to make choices and are held accountable for them. Here, on Day 20, I am asking you to think about Robert Frost and the words he wrote in 1915 when he said that there are two roads that diverge in a yellow wood, and we must choose which to take. Much like Frost's advice, I hope that you will choose the one less traveled by, for often it makes all the difference.

Reflection: "For the Lord himself will come down from heaven, with a loud command, with the voice of the archangel and with the trumpet call of God, and the dead in Christ will rise first. After that, we who are still alive and are left will be caught up together with them in the clouds to meet the Lord in the air. And so we will be with the Lord forever. Therefore encourage one another with these words " (1 Thessalonians 4:16-18).

Day 21

"There is nothing wrong with going to bed
with someone of your own sex.
People should be very free with sex,
they should draw the line at goats."

—Elton John

In a meeting in which the U.S. and the Swedes were discussing how we could help prevent AIDS, a member of the U.S. suggested teaching abstinence more in our school system.

The Swedes responded, "How will teenagers ever become loving, considerate, sexual partners if they do not practice?" There was a long silence in the room. That silence was the clash of values between cultures. The funny thing is that though the American media and pop culture give lots of publicity to shows such as *Jersey Shore*, in which sex is just sex without commitment or attachment, it is my personal opinion that many Americans still believe in the intimacy of sex, even if they are not practicing that belief. I say that because I teach college-age students and meet young girls every day who are struggling to figure out where they stand when it comes to sex.

For two years I worked as an assistant and then store manager for a well-known designer label clothing company. Though there were many things about the company that I did love, one example being the level of closeness and mentorship I got to experience with many of my teen workers, I had to resign after feeling a large conflict with what the company was promoting and my personal religious and moral beliefs. It is no secret that sex sells in this country, but the number of teenagers I meet who feel disconnected from God because of sexual immorality always encourages me. Satan is trying extremely hard to rid this country of any conscience, and at least from my conversations, I can tell that he has not completely succeeded, though he is clearly gaining ground and momentum. Satan would like us to live in a world in which sex is everywhere with anyone—girls with girls, guys with guys, completely casual, and even acceptable when two in-love married people have sex with other couples.

You see, Satan is no fool. He knows that when we destroy sex, we will eventually destroy marriage. In my opinion, it was no mistake that the very first institution Christ put in place on this world after Creation, even before the Sabbath, was marriage. God knew that in order for us to survive the temptations and trickery of the devil, two would be better than one. Marriage, when done correctly, is one of the most powerful and sacred bonds any two humans will experience in this world, and it serves as a motivational example for what Christ wants out of a relationship with us. From a faithful and Christ-rooted marriage, two people can create a faithful and Christ-rooted family. Typically, when marriage works, families work, and from productive families come productive disciples of Jesus Christ. You see, Satan was not God's number one student without reason. He is clever and has set out to destroy our race by first destroying our marriages, which destroys our families, and then he doesn't even have to do much about the products of those families, because by then we have so many personal issues that it makes understanding an ever-loving God quite difficult.

Satan knows what having several sexual partners outside of marriage does to a person's self-esteem, and also how the second we allow ourselves to start indulging in one carnal appetite, we have opened a window we may not be able to ever close. I don't think I hold the typical views about why we should abstain from sex outside of marriage. I believe that God is a loving and compassionate Father to us who simply knows when He created sex, what He created it for. Sex inside of marriage is crucial and extremely beneficial. When outside of marriage, and I can really only speak to the female perspective here, it will just leave you empty. I can't tell you how many girls I have spoken with who can't figure out why they have so much resentment and anger built up toward their great boyfriends. Girls trade sex for love. They think, *Oh, man, once I do this to him he is never going to let me go.* Eventually, though, you realize that you are giving the most intimate piece of yourself to someone who is not doing the same for you, and it hurts.

For men, their most intimate piece of themselves is their relationships. Many communication studies have taught that men bond with other men based off of shared activities. They create friendships because they both have similar interests, and that is typically the extent of their friendship. Without fail, my husband can go fishing with his best friend, and when he gets back from three or four hours of fellowship time and I ask him what new things are going on in his best friend's life, he has no clue. Perhaps this is why studies show that men rate their female friendships higher than they rate their male friendships. Because females know how to do one thing really well: build intimate relationships.

I tell my students every semester that the deepest intimacy you will ever achieve in a relationship is not sex but self-disclosure. The more you share about your inner thoughts and feelings with another person, the more connected to that person you will feel. A guy has best friends because they both like fishing, not because he is experiencing deep levels of self-disclosure with that friend. When a guy meets a girl, he is not going to fall madly in love with her because he has sex with her. The thing that will connect him to her will be his embarking on something so intimate that he has rarely done it before: self-disclosure. If a girl wants to get a guy to fall madly in love with her, or to feel intimately connected to her so much so that he can't let her go, she needs to build the bonds of a deep relationship. He will be rocked to his core. I am not being just a prude here —this is scientific.

Men are extremely loving creatures, perhaps sometimes more so than women. Studies also show that men are more likely to believe that their spouse and relationship are perfect than are women; they typically marry on the sole basis of love, and after a breakup, men have more fantasies and have a harder time getting over true love than women do. *Did you hear that?* Men spend more time fantasizing over a lost relationship than women do! Why? Because when a man connects intimately and then loses that connection, he has no other outlet to turn to. Whereas a woman will turn around and tell all six of her best girlfriends how she feels and then move on, men will suffer silently. And men, like women, need connection. They just don't know where to find it.

Men were created in the loving image of God, and unfortunately, because of "cowboy syndrome" in our society, they often no longer know how to express this side of themselves, but it is still there. Men are most vulnerable in intense emotional relationships, even more so than women, because they do not often experience them, even with their best male friends.

Women are relational. Where men report in communication what they did that day or what happened, women bond. We say how something made us feel. We build friendships off of shared intimacy and trust. Whereas men have typically only one or two extremely close relationships in their lives (one of which is almost always their mother), women have tons of close, intimate personal relationships. We do it without thinking.

The most personal thing a woman can give a man is sexual intimacy. Why? Because that is something that does not come naturally to her, even though she feels a deep emotional connection too. Relationships she does naturally. Self-disclosure is personal, but she also does this all the time, because she's good at self-disclosure. In reversal, the most intimate thing a man can give you is his relationship, or let you in to his inner thoughts and feelings. To have sex with a man without the commitment and relationship of marriage is the dumbest thing a female can do, because she is showing him all her cards while he is showing only a few of his.

You cannot exit that situation without feeling used and empty, because God knew that the most powerful way to fuse a man and a woman together was through sexual intimacy and committed relationship through self-disclosure. It is the only time a man and a woman are both giving each other their most vulnerable pieces. God took the two things both sexes hold dear and combined them through a commitment called marriage. This combination, when done in true love and trust, is explosive. A strong married couple can literally take on the world, because where one may stumble, the other, in love, will lift them up. Marriage is the ultimate symbolism of a loving, committed relationship and is still the standard of deep connection and emotional intimacy. Even the courts respect conversations shared between spouses, because marriage is the highest level of connectedness. Of course, then, Satan is working tirelessly to destroy it.

The thing is that Satan is also really good at using guilt to separate you from Christ. Remember, in my opinion, the number one goal of the devil is separation. He wants you to take yourself out of God's reach because he wants complete control. We cannot let guilt for what we have done in the past direct how we manage our futures. God does not care about your past; all He cares about is your willingness to allow Him to mold your present and your future.

I don't like to preach about sex too much and why it belongs in marriage, because I think people often just tune you out because it's a sermon they have heard before. I hope talking about it from a communication and gender study format may help explain why so many people talk about it. If you take away the spiritual implications of it, it is still a foolish thing to do. When you add in the spiritual implications, you are not only doing something foolish, but you are aiding Satan in his great deception. He would like you to believe that each issue is separate and one has nothing to do with the other, but they are all connected. Sex, marriage, family, and people are all directly correlated to one another. Satan doesn't want you to know that, though. He wants you to act on all carnal instinct until he destroys us from the inside out, one by one. The question is whether or not you are going to let him.

Reflection: "Marriage should be honored by all, and the marriage bed kept pure, for God will judge the adulterer and all the sexually immoral" (Hebrews 13:4).

Day 22

When my uncle died, I sat on the phone with my mother as she remembered various things about him. "I remember going to his house with him once as a teenager, and he had just got paid from work. When we got to his home, I was astonished, because he took his checks and cash out of his pockets, opened the closet door, and tossed it all in. He then closed the door and continued talking to me as if nothing had just happened. In his closet were lots of money and uncashed checks, and I remember just standing there thinking, *Who does that?*"

I giggled for a moment as I thought about my uncle. He counted his pennies, and everyone knew that he didn't like to spend too many of them. My sister is the exact same way. In fact, when my mom said, "Who does that?" I thought about how strong genes must run through DNA, because my sister does that. I hate when she says she doesn't have any money, because what she really means is that she doesn't have any money in her wallet. She does, however, have checks hidden in various locations and probably doesn't even remember where they are anymore.

I bought her a gift card last year for her birthday and just happened to be going through her wallet to get something the other day and found my gift card, along with probably 10 others, presents she has kept tucked away in her wallet for a rainy day. What annoyed me is that the store she had all the gift cards from was a store we had just spent lots of money at, buying decorations for our new residences. When I asked her why she didn't use the gift card I had bought her when we were just at the store last week, she said, "I forgot I had it."

When we were kids, I would eat all my Halloween candy the second I got it. Literally, a bag of candy was reduced to mere wrappers within 24 to 48 hours, depending on how big the score. My sister, in contrast, would hoard all of her candy and not even find it till almost the next Halloween, when it would be all old and moldy. It would make me so mad because naturally when I would run out of my candy I would ask her for some of hers, and she'd never share.

"It's my candy," she'd say. "You ate yours."

She was right, but it didn't sit well, since I knew that her candy was just going to rot in that bag. Even recently I asked her for a roll of toilet paper because she lives right next door to me and I didn't feel like going to the store. She gave it to me, but I could tell she didn't want to.

"Toilet paper is expensive," she said when she handed me the roll. My sister does not understand how someone could even run out of toilet paper, because she would never let that happen. It's funny because her lack of sharing may annoy me, but I am certain that my lack of saving often annoys her.

Saving is a good thing, but what is the point if you never get to use the very items you are saving? When it comes to God and our relationship with Him, don't save any of it. I have been finding myself in more and more conversations about God with my friends than I ever did before. When they bring up moral issues, I like to somehow interject something about God or the Bible into the conversation and just see if I get any bites. It's funny because it is completely contradictory to the rest of my personality, but for some reason when it comes to God, it is not easy for me to talk about Him. I feel really vulnerable when I express to others face to face about how in love with Him I am, or how convicted of various things I have become through our time together. I don't want them to reject Him or what I am saying, because, in part, I will feel as though they are rejecting me.

I have to tell you, though, that the moments that others do receive what I am saying and start discussing their relationship with God with me is a high like no other. In those moments I feel so connected because I get to experience God with someone else. While reading *40 Days of Prayer,* by Alvin VanderGriend, I had a moment in which I felt that he was really speaking to just me when he talked about Christianity needing fellowship in order to reach its highest potential. The truth is I love writing about God, but it does not come as natural for me to start up a conversation about God, even though once I am in one it is almost euphoric. Fellowship is certainly not my best attribute. Ever since I read his book, however, I have really tried to put myself in more fellowship environments. I started a Bible study with a few friends this past year, and I really enjoyed myself. We meant to meet for only an hour, but somehow time would lose itself and we'd sit with one another till midnight.

I think when it comes to God, I can be like my uncle Larry with his checks or my sister with her Halloween candy; I save Him and like to keep Him all to myself. Fellowship is powerful, though for more than one reason. Not only can we learn from others' experiences and feel strength by our numbers, but it also helps to hold ourselves accountable by expressing struggles to other sincere Christians. It helps to push past guilt and move toward reconciliation with Christ when we share with someone we trust what our problems are. I started doing that with a friend of mine through one of my Bible studies, and it has brought me a lot of peace.

In Matthew 25:14-30 we see the parable of the talents. I think Jesus, like me, loved stories. He often used them to get a message across. This particular story tells us that a man was going on a trip and needed the servants of his household to take care of things while he was away. Now, before I go much further, I should explain what a talent was. A talent was not a measure of money or coins, but was a precious metal comparable to silver. Scholars believe one talent was worth more than $1,000.

So the man going on a trip calls in all his servants. To the first servant he gave five talents. This is then like handing him more than $5,000. This servant took his money and wanted to do his part to add to it. He put that money to work and ended up doubling it. To the second servant the master gave two talents, so a little more than $2,000. Now, I am not sure why he gave $5,000 to the first and only $2,000 to the second. Perhaps he knew his servants well and knew how much each could handle. This second servant also does a great work and doubles his money. To the third servant the master gives one talent, or $1,000. He wanted to provide an opportunity to this servant to double his money as well. Instead of doubling it, though, he hoarded it. He dug a hole, put the talent in it, and buried it.

After a long while the master returned. Some have speculated that this trip is symbolic of Jesus' ascension to heaven and then return to earth to call home His saints. If so, Jesus comes back, calls us up, and wants to know what we did with the beautiful talents He gave us. When Jesus hears that the first servant doubled his original endowment, He is excited! He says, "Well done, good and faithful servant! You have been faithful with a few things; I will put you in charge of many things. Come and share your master's happiness!" (Matthew 25:21).

So if this is meant to be Jesus asking us at the end of our lives about what we have done with what He gave us, we can see that if we make an attempt to double it, cultivate it, and share it, Christ is beyond pleased. That is exactly what He expects from us. The man who tells about what he did with his two talents receives the same response as the accolades given to the first servant. We see here that it doesn't matter if you have done less than someone else, as long as you have made the best efforts with the gifts and talents you were given. When we come to our last servant, however, the one who dug the hole and hid the talent, the servant simply returns to the master what the master originally gave him. At this the master is very angry and refers to the man as "wicked."

Don't save God so much so that you never get to share Him with someone else. God has given you something, and you need to figure out how to use it. In fact, your entire purpose in life depends on it. Fellowship is a blessing. Christ is our greatest treasure, and unlike checks or Halloween candy, it's OK if you share Him with someone who doesn't have any left. Christ and love are probably the only things in this world where the more you give out, the more you get back.

Reflection: "Give, and it will be given to you. A good measure, pressed down, shaken together and running over, will be poured into your lap. For with the measure you use, it will be measured to you" (Luke 6:38).

Day 23

"I'm texting and on Facebook. Texting + Facebook = textbook.
Therefore, I am STUDYING!"

—Unknown

In a religion class I took in college, I was prompted to try fasting for a day. I had never fasted the whole day before, so I decided that I would take the challenge head-on. I have had a very sensitive time clock when it comes to my next meal since I was a child. I literally get physically faint and sick if I don't eat breakfast, lunch, and dinner. I decided the only way I could fast would be if I told myself that at midnight I could eat. So I bought a gallon of grape juice, and on the day I had designated, I started my fast. In the past few days prior to my fast, I decided to add one extra element: I was also going to fast from technology.

I suppose I shouldn't say technology, because I was planning to spend my day using the computer, just not the Internet. I had a book I needed to finish and was suffering from a slight writer's block, so my fast was to break the block, finish the book, and focus on the mission I believe God has called me to, which is writing, but without any distractions. I turned off my TV, turned off my iPod, and stayed logged out of my Myspace and Facebook accounts. That day, in between giant glasses of grape juice, I wrote the last couple chapters necessary to complete the book I had been pouring my heart and soul into for the past few years. It actually is the first book I even wrote, though to this day I still haven't taken the time to clean it up and repitch it to publishers after its initial rejection.

For three years or so I had labored intensely over that book and just couldn't get myself to finish it. I had mapped out my chapters and knew where I wanted the story to go, but I just hadn't been able to get myself to see it through. I had a lot of distractions at that time in my life. In undergraduate school I actually had friends that called and I spoke to on a regular basis. I had TV shows to watch and an online persona to attain.

My husband doesn't care for Facebook because he says no one ever writes on his wall. I try to explain to him that social networking systems such as Facebook don't just run themselves; you have to put in to get out. You can't expect to just make an account and have instantaneous daily comments unless your last name is Kardashian. I poured years of witty postings and statuses into my Facebook before I got that ship sailing. I regularly posted new photos and put my work in commenting on other people's before I really started to reap the satisfaction of seeing 32 "likes" on any given update. It takes serious cyber social commitment to ensure your page is popular on everyone's news feed, and my husband simply doesn't understand that. The one day I decided to turn everything else off and turn God up, I finished my book in a breeze. The words flowed from me like poetry, because I was in the zone and I wasn't distracted.

Today, as we near the last week of our 30 days together, I really charge you to remember why we started here in the first place. We are living in a culture that is so easily oversaturated with instant communication and gratification that we no longer even turn our cell phones off during a church service. God is waiting patiently for you to log into Him. My daily devotional readings, paired with the reading of Scripture, have been a life-altering experience. If there is one thing I can promise you, it's that if you are feeling disconnected in your current walk with God, spending time alone with Him in your mornings will disrupt everything Satan has been putting in place.

My husband often tells me that the highest he has ever felt spiritually is when he served in Chuuk, Micronesia, as a student missionary. While he was there he taught Bible courses and literally had nothing to do with his days other than study the Word of God and enjoy time spent in God's nature. It is so much harder to connect spiritually when we have the distractions of life available at our disposal, but I know for a fact that we can feel a missionary high right here at home if we only have the willpower to turn the rest off and plug back in to God's outlet. If you need to call it a fast, fast from technology for a day and allow yourself to be refreshed by Christ.

Just as you have to eventually stop and reconnect your iPod to its charger in order to keep hearing music, we must take the time daily to charge up on Christ. And though I pray that this book and this page will give you a spark throughout your day, I can't stress enough how much you need to lace it with your own study of Scripture in order to start the fire necessary to finish this race. God has a plan that can be accomplished only by your personality, your experiences, and your action. I can't fulfill your mission, your mother can't fulfill your mission, and your private school friends can't fulfill your mission. This is something He has called just for you, and it doesn't matter how impressive your sound-track list—if you don't fire up those batteries, no one is going to hear your music. Remember that if we want to finish this race and stand tall when Christ returns as the groom to take His bride, we are expected to reflect the image of Christ fully.

I once heard a story about a group of women who were experiencing Christ through community. They were having a Bible study and were going over the book of Malachi. They hit Malachi 3:3 and were puzzled at the description given. The verse reads, "He will sit as a refiner and purifier of silver; he will purify the Levites and refine them like gold and silver." They were confused by the verse and wondered what this said about God's character and persona.

I like that part of the story already, because this is how I have been training myself to read Scripture. Read a couple verses and then stop and actually ponder just what that meant or is saying about Christ. What is the message to be gained from this verse?

One of the women in the group decided to take it upon herself to find the answer for the others. She said she would visit a silversmith and ask if she could observe the process of refining silver. She made an appointment, and a few days later was visiting a silversmith. While there, she chose not to explain to the man why she wanted to understand the process; she simply left it with him thinking she was just curious about how the process worked.

While she watched him work, she asked a few questions as he placed the silver in the fire. He explained to the woman that in order to refine silver, one must place it in the hottest part of the fire in order to rid the silver of any impurities. She watched the tiny piece of silver centered in such strong flames, and she thought about Christ holding us, like silver, through the toughest of adversities.

She asked the silversmith if it was important for him to sit there in front of the fire while the silver was refining. He answered her that not only did he have to sit there holding the silver, but he also had to keep his eyes on it completely the entire time. He told her that if he didn't keep his eyes on it intensely, that if he looked away for just a moment and the silver was left in the fire too long, it would all be destroyed. She then marveled at the words of God she had read in Malachi 3:3. She smiled as she thought about this picture of God that she was just now seeing more clearly, how meticulous He is, how loving and protective.

"And how do you know when the silver is done?" she asked after a few moments of silent awe at what she had just discovered.

"Oh, that part is easy," the man responded. "The silver is done when I can see my reflection in it."

Ellen White said in *Testimonies for the Church:* "I saw that God is purifying and proving His people. He will refine them as gold, until the dross is consumed and His image is reflected in them" (vol. 1, p. 355).

God would like to use you to accomplish a great work. If you allow Him, He will use you. You may feel some fire, but do not worry; He is holding you, eyes never blinking, face never turning away. Jesus, the one whom they called Christ, has a plan for you. But first, He must see His reflection.

Reflection: "Like newborn babies, crave pure spiritual milk, so that by it you may grow up in your salvation" (1 Peter 2:2).

Day 24

"You don't really understand human nature unless you know why a child on a merry-go-round will wave at his parents every time around, and why his parents will always wave back."

—William D. Tammeus

Something extraordinary happens when you become a parent. It's like something changes, and all your thoughts and prayers are centered on one person. I once heard someone say that having a child is like living the rest of your life with your heart walking around outside of your chest. I'm currently only seven months pregnant, but my husband and I are both already overwhelmed at times by the rush of emotions that comes when we think of our daughter's entrance into this world.

When I was a little girl, I don't think I spent too much time fantasizing about having a family of my own. I dreamed about writing novels or acting in movies. When I got older and became interested in boys, I did dream about what my wedding or my husband would be like, but still didn't feel much maternal interest in a future family. When I met Seth, the one thing I remember thinking was that he was without a doubt the only man I had ever fantasized about having children with. There was something so sweet and genuine in his soul that made me certain that this man would be an incredible father, and for the first time ever I came to believe that I could be a good mom.

I have said before that my parents were exceptional. My prayer is that I can fulfill my parental role half as well as they did. I think the crucial technique in their parenting style was that they never cared if we liked them. "My job is not for you to like me," my dad always said. "My job is to make sure you get to heaven."

All the incredible biblical patriarchs we can read about in Scripture who were righteous in the Lord and yet failed as parents amazes me. Eli, the priest who took in Samuel after Hannah dedicated him to the Lord, is probably the first that comes to my mind. He was a strong man of faith and loved his sons greatly, perhaps so much that he could not correct their bad behavior, and because of their abuse of priestly power, much faith in Christ was lost in Israel.

First Samuel 2:22-26 tells us the story: "Now Eli, who was very old, heard about everything his sons were doing to all Israel and how they slept with the women who served at the entrance to the tent of meeting. So he said to them, 'Why do you do such things? I hear from all the people about these wicked deeds of yours. No, my sons; the report I hear spreading among the Lord's people is not good. If one person sins against another, God may mediate for the offender; but if anyone sins against the Lord, who will intercede for them?' His sons, however, did not listen to their father's rebuke, for it was the Lord's will to put them to death. And the boy Samuel continued to grow in stature and in favor with the Lord and with people."

In verse 27 a man of God comes to Eli and rebukes him for what he has allowed to go on. You see, Eli should have stripped his sons of any right to continue serving God in such a high level of office. But his love for his sons clouded his judgment.

And in verse 29 the man of God says, "Why do you scorn my sacrifice and offering that I prescribed for my dwelling? Why do you honor your sons more than me by fattening yourselves on the choice parts of every offering made by my people Israel?"

Verses 30-34 conclude, "Therefore the Lord, the God of Israel, declares: 'I promised that members of your family would minister before me forever.' But now the Lord declares: 'Far be it from me! Those who honor me I will honor, but those who despise me will be disdained. The time is coming when I will cut short your strength and the strength of your priestly house, no one in it will reach old age, and you will see distress in my dwelling. Although good will be done to Israel, no one in your family line will ever reach old age. Every one of you that I do not cut off from my altar I will spare only to destroy your sight and sap your strength, and all your descendants will die in the prime of life.

"'And what happens to your two sons, Hophni and Phinehas, will be a sign to you—they will both die on the same day. I will raise up for myself a faithful priest, who will do according to what is in my heart and mind. I will firmly establish his priestly house, and they will minister before my anointed one always.'"

Now, what surprises me about all of this is that Samuel, who grows up literally watching the mistakes of Eli, does similar things with his own children. He still had a hard time raising his own sons.

Another example is David. David loved Absalom greatly, and was also a man who stood in high favor with God, and yet Absalom, without David's correction of his poor behavior, tries to destroy all that David had built.

Love is a good thing, but as a parent, love without correction can do more harm than good. In this we see a powerful lesson about why Christ must put out the sin of His children, even though He loves them dearly. This is not Him being bloodthirsty, but at some point He has to stop the wicked before they destroy the good.

Parenting is the hardest job you will ever have, and striking a balance between love and discipline can be difficult, but is still necessary. Sometimes we don't understand why God allows certain things to happen to us. We get angry at Him for not handing us life on a silver platter or making us work hard to get various things accomplished. The thing is, though, that God is not just a God of great honor and integrity; He is also an incredible dad. His goal is not to make our lives comfortable, but to ensure that we reunite with Him in heaven. When we learn from our mistakes and dig deeper after failure, He is helping mold in us a pure character that can withstand all the evil and temptation Satan is foaming at the mouth to put in our path. My relationship with my father has helped me greatly in understanding my relationship with Christ. God is the best parent, and we are so lucky to call Him Abba, Daddy.

The average parent, though, doesn't have to hang from a cross as their children put nails into their wrists. They also don't have to sit silently as they endure watching that same child deny their Creator's very existence either in word or by action. You see, being Christ is like living your life walking around with your heart beating outside of your chest. It is strange that our heart is the only organ, that I can think of, that we can hear while it's working. Perhaps this is a friendly message from God to its holder that He made that heart, and with each heavy powerful thump comes a reminder that He is madly in love with you; and until the thumps cease and the noise silences, He will stand beside you patiently waiting for you to only accept His presence.

It is often said that God speaks through a still small whisper. I'd like to think that He is also speaking through the thuds of our chest cavities. The next time you are alone, in the stillness of the quiet, take a few moments to do nothing but listen to your heartbeat. You'll never hear silence quite that loud.

Reflection: "But because of his great love for us, God, who is rich in mercy, made us alive with Christ even when we were dead in transgressions—it is by grace you have been saved" (Ephesians 2:4, 5).

Day 25

Sometimes I catch myself thinking back to when I was a child and things were simple. I was a better form of myself then, innocent. For the most part, I did as I was told and listened to those who had authority over me. I believed that people were trustworthy and that the only thing scary in life was the possibility of monsters hiding underneath my bed. Little things made my day back then. If my mom bought me a doughnut while grocery shopping at Meijer, I was smitten with excitement for the rest of the day. When my daddy told me I was pretty, I believed him, and didn't need any further confirmation on my identity.

On Saturday nights my parents would make us nachos and virgin piña coladas, and it was my favorite day of the entire week. I didn't need friends or toys or cable with a thousand channels. I was genuinely happy with nachos and the companionship of my family. I always felt safe as long as we were all together, and I had such a sense of peace because of all the things I didn't know and all the important lessons I had yet to learn.

Everything was easy then. Monsters ran away when you turned the lights on, and anytime you fell down you were instantly pressed tight into the arms of someone bigger. You never had to cry alone, and if you had a rough night you could crawl into your parents' bed and they'd make room for you because there was nowhere that you didn't belong.

Things change when you get older. You discover that a lot of people are not trustworthy, and that perfectly good hearts get broken. You discover that just because your daddy thinks you're pretty doesn't mean the other girls and boys in your class agree with him. You learn that monsters stay even when the lights are on, and when you fall down you have to lift yourself back up. Suddenly the world isn't as safe and peaceful, and you find a lot of places that you just don't belong. Suddenly you have to tuck yourself in at night, and during scary dreams there is no bigger bed to crawl into. Life is hard and nothing is easy, and sometimes it all changes too fast.

We find ourselves making choices we shouldn't have and doing things we shouldn't do. We are anything but innocent, and with each step forward we pull the weight of the past. We are bombarded with thoughts and images of who we were and who we could have been, and it's typically nothing like the reflection in the mirror of who we are right now. Often the heaviest guilt is not for what we are doing, but what we have done. In the transition of child to adult, we lost our peace and can't help feeling a bit tattered and damaged amid all that we've lost and the new selves we have gained.

This is, in my mind, the beauty of baptism. It is a chance for your spirit to be wiped clean of all that was. A chance to again become a child, innocent and trusting in the plan of your Savior. Suddenly the only affirmation we need again is for our Father to see us as beautiful, and we will believe it. Baptism is God's greatest act of mercy, literally an opportunity to be born again, to start over, only this time not at peace because of all that you don't know, but at peace because of all you have learned. I was baptized in the ocean two days after I married my husband. It was one of the best days of my life, and at 24 I became a child again in the eyes of Christ. It took me a long time to finally submit my will completely to Christ through baptism. It was an act that I took, and take, very seriously. On Day 25 of our journey together, if God is calling you to submit to His authority through baptism, or rebaptism, pray fervently, take it seriously, and then move toward action. It will literally be the first day of the rest of your life.

In Matthew 3:13-17 we see the story of Christ's baptism. "Then Jesus came from Galilee to the Jordan to be baptized by John. But John tried to deter him, saying, 'I need to be baptized by you, and do you come to me?'" (verses 13, 14).

The first thing I would like to note here is that John the Baptist has just spent his entire life preaching and preparing the way for Jesus Christ. When it comes to radical discipleship, we see that in John the Baptist. Now, when Jesus comes and John is able to fulfill one of the greatest moments of his life, he begins to refuse. John does not feel it is appropriate for him to baptize Jesus. "It is You who should be baptizing me!" he says.

John feels unqualified to do the task that Christ has allowed him to fulfill. This speaks volumes to me, because how many times have I spent all my energy trying to do something for God, trying to make something of this life that I have, and when He allows me to fulfill some of my mission, I suddenly feel too small? When He opens a potential door, I feel unqualified. You, like John, have a mission. Jesus does not call the qualified; He qualifies the called.

"Jesus replied, 'Let it be so now; it is proper for us to do this to fulfill all righteousness.' Then John consented. As soon as Jesus was baptized, he went up out of the water. At that moment heaven was opened, and he saw the Spirit of God descending like a dove and lighting on him. And a voice from heaven said, 'This is my Son, whom I love; with him I am well pleased'" (verses 15-17).

My next question here is Why did Jesus need to be baptized? He was blameless, sinless; for what did He need to atone? Christ was baptized not for His sins but for ours. Through baptism we see Him announce the beginning of His ministry. I believe God has called every single one of us to use our life in some way to better His ministry. You don't have to be a pastor or an evangelist to minister. In my opinion, friendship can be one of the most powerful ministries. Authentic displays of Christianity will serve as someone's altar call. Use your gifts, whatever those may be, to serve God and live as a testament to His Word. Again, before Jesus starts His ministry, He is baptized. If Jesus' life is to be our example, what can we take from His need to be baptized before beginning His ministry?

I was about to write a lovely conclusion here, answering the question that I have just posed, but I am reminded that sometimes the only thing better than hearing a beautiful, well-put answer is coming up with it yourself.

Reflection: "I baptize you with water for repentance. But after me will come one who is more powerful than I, whose sandals I am not worthy to carry. He will baptize you with the Holy Spirit and fire" (Matthew 3:11).

Day 26

"Time is passing. Yet, for the United States of America,
there will be no forgetting September 11.
We will remember every rescuer who died in honor.
We will remember every family that lives in grief. We will remember
the fire and ash, the last phone calls, the funerals of the children."
—George W. Bush, November 11, 2001

My husband was asked to lead the worship at his work this past week. When I asked him what he was going to speak about, he said he was thinking about discussing the first time he experienced God, and how his life had changed since.

My husband first experienced God after smoking marijuana in his itty-bitty high school's gym locker room got him dismissed from school for the rest of the year. He said that while he was home, overhearing various tales about him from the rumor mill, he lost himself in the terrible image others had created of him.

When I say itty-bitty school, I am not using this term lightly. My husband's church school class had maybe 10 students, so when I say he felt as though everyone in the whole school was talking about him, they literally probably were. To make matters worse, my husband's mother taught at the same school, so not only did he embarrass himself, but also, even worse, he humiliated his mother.

He had the rest of the year to spend in homeschool, thinking about what he had done and feeling like the village idiot. Actually, when he told me the story, my first response was "What kind of idiot smokes pot in a gym locker room where there are only a handful of students, so it really would take only a matter of minutes to figure out who was the culprit?"

At any rate, his experience with Christ was much like my own, in spite of foolishness; Christ still loved him, and met him where he was. He went on to explain that for the first time in his life, after meeting Jesus as his friend, he found a sense of value in who he was. He said that up until that point, he had felt pretty worthless. He didn't feel smart, and in an Adventist school system where athletics is not valued, your brain actually is. Now, I will insert my own commentary here, because my husband is actually brilliant, but the beauty of his brilliance, at least that caught my eye, is that it is exceeded only by his humility. It is not hard for Seth to give God all the glory for any successes that come his way. He is one of those people with very little self-faith who operate solely on the faith that Christ is who He says He is, and will use us according to His will, in spite of our failures.

I love that about him, because I am the opposite. I have always liked myself. I've never thought I was perfect, but I had parents who did a good job of making me feel pretty close. I am naturally confident in the things I do because I know myself. I know what I am good at and what I am not. Where Seth's struggle is in believing he is worthy to do something on God's behalf, my struggle is in not completely taking things into my own hands and submitting to complete dependence on God. That and guilt of past indiscretions that I know have humiliated the best Friend I have ever had: Christ.

I often joke with my husband that he is like Moses, and I am like David. God loves me solely because I love Him so much. I sincerely want to be on fire for Him, so I am like that kid sister He can't seem to get rid of, and so He loves me because He sees how desperately I want to hang out with Him. Seth, on the other hand, like Moses, is humble, and God sees him and knows He can use him greatly because he will always give credit where credit is due. God loved both David and Moses earnestly, but humility is a powerful tool in the hands of Christ. It was Moses whom Christ has already resurrected, and also Moses who meets Christ in His final hours on earth at the Mount of Transfiguration.

After my husband finished talking to me and went to go shower, I sat on the couch thinking about what he had said. He said he'd been changed since he met Christ, because he never saw value in himself until he found value solely because he knew who it was that loved him. That changed him, and ever since, though he still made mistakes, he earnestly tried to do better because he didn't want to let God down. He couldn't believe that this great big God loved the village idiot, and it made him want to be smarter. It made him want to succeed for Christ's sake.

I started wondering how my life had been changed since I met Christ. If you ask yourself that question and can't think of a real definite answer, you have to wonder if you have even met Him yet at all. Meeting Christ should shake you. Even if the moment was more of a gradual process, you should still see aftereffects that are burned into your mind and from which you've never been the same. It should be almost like September 11, where people ask you where you were when it happened, and suddenly your mind takes you right back to that moment and you smell the same smells and see the same imagery. If it isn't like that, maybe you're still waiting to meet Him. Sure you may know who He is, read about Him, hear about Him, and talk about Him, but have you shaken His hand for yourself?

In my life I feel that I have always known of Christ, though perhaps He would not say He has always known me. For me, it was not in despair or agony, but more so a culmination of all the small whispers He'd been pressing lightly to my ears. I was getting ready and looking in the mirror, and I finally decided to give in. I realized that I couldn't trust in my own abilities, and I needed to submit my will to His. I said aloud to God, "I submit to Your authority."

It's funny because, at the time, it didn't seem that so much had changed; but looking back, I realize that I have completely given up on the plans that I had for myself, and have been following His leading. I was going to be a journalist. Unlike normal little girls who want to be princesses, my first-grade diary was filled with aspirations to be like my hero Barbara Walters. In high school, to make fun of my dreams, many of my guy friends called me Oprah, but I didn't care.

Much because of that day in my room, I am not a journalist, nor do I secretly want to be. God had plans for me, and I honestly can say that I wouldn't have chosen the path I am on now, had it not been for His guidance, though I have never felt more assured and at peace with what I am doing with my life. I don't think my story on meeting God is as interesting as getting caught smoking pot in my high school gym, but it's my moment, and it makes me smile to look at who I was and where I was going in comparison to where God has taken me. I couldn't ask for a better job, creative outlet, husband, or soon-to-be life as a mother, and I owe all that to my moment when, in sincerity, I vocalized a few words to Christ.

How terrible the burden must feel to be God. To have in mind such incredible ideas and plans for someone who refuses to allow you to suggest them. To be watching and loving someone desperately who keeps picking their own path, forcing their own way, and missing this incredible purpose and design for their life's work. When I met Christ, I also met a great sense of relief. I met peace. He has a plan for me, and as long as I spend my time connecting to His life source, He will continue leading.

I know I write a lot about God's plan for you and figuring out what that is, but I have to explain that I do this because the burden on my heart is that He is trying to raise a generation ready to claim their roles in this last-day ministry. I believe that God's plan for my life is to advocate youth to respond to this call. He is coming back. He is coming back soon, and Satan is busy readying his forces to go to battle. My worry is that we are not as busy. We need to be preparing our camp. We need to be worried about casualties and doing everything within our power to ensure that not one soul within our reach is lost.

Recently, while studying Revelation, I have felt compelled to make sure that I have done everything in my power to ensure that my family is prepared to meet Him. Evangelism is important, but our first concern should be right in our own homes. When Christ returns, we will answer for all that we did and did not say, and the loss of someone in my own family is simply not a price I am willing to pay. If every Christian simply took account for those within his or her own family, we would see conversion ripple across the world. Start with your family, and then continue making waves.

When we go to heaven for that thousand years before coming back to claim the earth from Satan and his company, we will notice who is not there. We will look around and see that our loved ones or our friends that we could have reached but didn't are not in attendance. We will spend that thousand years understanding why someone whom in our earthly lives we loved so dearly is not with us, is not also bonding with Christ. I cannot bear the thought of going to heaven without my sister. I cannot bear the thought of going to heaven without my brother, my nephews, my parents, grandparents, aunts, uncles, cousins, and, heaven forbid, my husband or daughter.

The more time I have been spending with God, the more real this all has become for me, and the more urgent this message of present truth. I lay this burden on your shoulders as well because you have already been reading this book. Therefore, you have made a conscious effort to start cultivating your spiritual self. There are no coincidences, only Christ-incidences, and you and I have met for a reason. It is time to join forces and commit to meeting Christ. We need to commit to allowing Him to clean us up from the inside out and use us to accomplish His objective. Christ is feverishly working around the clock to raise a generation. Satan also has been busy, but have you?

Whether you're like Moses or David, you've got to meet Him if you haven't already. You can't waste another minute. You have no idea of all the great things He has planned for you, if you'll first just submit to His will. If you have met Him, reflect on that moment you first did, look at where you were and how far you've come, and keep moving forward. And if you have met Him and somewhere along your walk you feel as though you've lost hold of His hand, it's OK, because God is always the easiest person to spot in the crowd. He's that guy at the airport waving His hands back and forth in utter excitement, spotted instantly because of His ear-to-ear smile. In His hands is a sign with not only your name on it, but also a message that He's been holding up since before He ever told the story of the prodigal son: "My Child, Welcome Home."

Reflection: "The son said to him, 'Father, I have sinned against heaven and against you. I am no longer worthy to be called your son.' But the father said to his servants, 'Quick! Bring the best robe and put it on him. Put a ring on his finger and sandals on his feet. Bring the fattened calf and kill it. Let's have a feast and celebrate. For this son of mine was dead and is alive again; he was lost and is found.' So they began to celebrate" (Luke 15:21-24).

Day 27

"This is our temporary home; it's not where we belong. "
—Carrie Underwood, "Temporary Home"

I found myself daydreaming this morning during a class. My professor played the hymn "Heav'n Is My Home," written by Thomas R. Taylor, that was first published in 1836. The words, though old, struck a chord in my heart as they flashed up on a large projector screen. One stanza says, "I'm but a stranger here, Heav'n is my home; Earth is a desert drear, Heav'n is my home."

As I read those words, I was moved. What if we really believed that earth had nothing for us, and that heaven was our home? How would that notion impact the way we live our lives? As Christians, we are taught to believe that, we say we believe that, but what if we actually did? How would it change the way we interact not only with Christ but with other Christians? How would it change the jobs we had, or the things we did, or the way we spent our free time?

I have said it before, but important things bear repeating: One of Satan's biggest weapons in his arsenal to claim your life is just to keep you occupied doing anything and everything else, good or bad, that distracts you from Christ. He knows that all he has to do is keep you busy getting caught up in the tidings and pleasures or bills of this world, and he will claim you. When we believe that earth is our home, the battle is over, and Satan has won.

When Christ said in Matthew 24:37, "As it was in the days of Noah, so it will be at the coming of the Son of Man," He was saying that just as Noah had spent his life preaching about an approaching flood, and just as the people had witnessed the animals marching two by two into a giant ark and had not thought to themselves, *Hey, maybe this guy is onto something,* so it will be in the last days. Just as they were too busy to recognize their own damnation, too busy eating, drinking, and giving of one another in marriage, so will we be too busy to recognize Christ's second coming. Just as in the days of Noah, with or without you that door is going to close.

Unlike then, however, now we have experienced Christ's first coming to earth as the Word became flesh. We have heard His testimonies, read about His miracles, and seen much of prophecy being fulfilled. What you are feeling right now is raindrops, and instead of looking around wondering if you will have time to get your house in order or your name in lights, we should be running toward the ark doors and begging to get on board.

I read a vision Ellen White was given, printed in *Early Writings* (a book, by the way, that I strongly recommend reading, as she explains what present truth is in the end days and how we can share it), in which she talks about seeing Jesus in heaven and He turned His face from her in despair. She saw this because she said when she first started receiving visions she had a hard time delivering them because people were not liking some of the harsh realities she was being shown. She found herself softening down some of the harder words, and God gave her this vision to show her that He was not pleased. She says that seeing His face downcast from her was the most painful experience; she couldn't speak and wanted so desperately to run into her Savior's arms and ask Him to let her do it all over. She is released from the vision and promises herself to never again soften God's message for fear of hurting feelings, because the message is urgent and God is moving. (See p. 76.) I too believe that God has a message for us still today that is incredibly urgent.

The truth is, I do not feel like a stranger on this earth, but I can honestly say that the more connected to God I become, the more disconnected I feel from where I am, and until this morning while listening to that old hymn sung in my classroom, I didn't really understand why. The key to believing that heaven is your home is believing that Jesus is your Father. Once we accept that, we must connect ourselves with Him so tightly that we are forced to remember that this world, aside from our mission in Christ, has nothing for us. Once we really digest that thought, suddenly not only does life make sense, but death also makes sense. You are still here. You are still breathing. There is still a message to be given, and that message is still urgent.

Take it from me, a person who has spent a lot of time, sweat, and agony planning every step I needed to take to make sure I was successful in this life. I wanted to push through school and get my Ph.D. before I was 30. I wanted to work hard, make money, and put myself in a position in which I could support my family, regardless of whether I married a lawyer or a plumber. I wanted to win pageants, be the homecoming queen, and write novels that became best sellers. For most of my life, up until recent points, I have pushed and pulled and worked to do many of those things, and suddenly when I really started to connect with Christ, none of it mattered. We should exert our most energy getting ourselves to where God wants us to be. For me, that hasn't been in winning pageants or writing books competitive with *Harry Potter*, and so I have had to forget my plans and submit to His.

I too cannot bear to ever meet with Christ and, instead of seeing His face elated at my sight, watch as He turns that beautiful face downward and cannot meet my eyes. My friend Cortney always says, "I'd rather my parents be furious with me than disappointed." I think we really underestimate the level to which we will be held accountable for the way we have impacted or not impacted the lives of those around us. You cannot just accept God and keep Him to yourself, or sing about Him in your church, or talk about Him with your church friends in your church pews or at your Bible studies. You must also step outside of your comfort zone.

I am realizing more and more that just because our church friends went to Christian school with us doesn't make them Christians. Because you were born Seventh-day Adventist doesn't make you Seventh-day Adventist. Your parent's religiosity isn't going to do squat for you on judgment day. You have got to meet Jesus for yourself, then you have got to share Him with those closest to you, and then you have got to share Him with anyone He allows to cross your path. You cannot call yourself a Christian if no one else would. There is a message to be delivered and there are people who are spiritually starving, and I know a church that is full of fat members. We have got to share. Lately I have grown more and more in tune with Christ, and as this is happening, I am growing more aware that heaven is my home. I want to be a stranger here, because heaven is my home.

Today I will end this journey with you with a question, because I do not have all the answers for you, and every reader should personalize this question and be able to develop their own response. That question is: How would you change your life and your path at this moment, if you really believed that you were simply a stranger here and that heaven was your home?

Reflection: "All these people were still living by faith when they died. They did not receive the things promised; they only saw them and welcomed them from a distance, admitting that they were foreigners and strangers on earth. People who say such things show that they are looking for a country of their own. If they had been thinking of the country they had left, they would have had opportunity to return. Instead, they were longing for a better country—a heavenly one. Therefore God is not ashamed to be called their God, for he has prepared a city for them" (Hebrews 11:13-16).

Day 28

"By failing to prepare, you are preparing to fail."
—Benjamin Franklin

My husband and I put up our daughter London's crib last night. We got a white one, and her bedding is decorated with pink ballerina teddy bears. As a child, I often daydreamed about having a canopy over my bed. I thought I would feel like a princess if I could only go to sleep amid light-pink flowing material that surrounded my bed like a hazy mist. For some reason my parents never got me a canopy.

To this day, my grandmother still talks about the pony she wanted as a little girl and never got. I'm sure if she reads this, her eyebrows will raise, and in her memories an empty box will appear for the pony she always wanted and never did get. That canopy was my pony. I am sure one day I will be 80 years old, and when I think back to all the fond memories of my youth, somewhere like a dark passenger the thought of the canopy I never owned will trickle into my mind and I'll frown.

I'm not very artsy or creative when it comes to design or colors or really anything artistic. My brain is in overdrive when it comes to words or doing something outside the box, but I am definitely deficient when it comes to anything else in that arena. I am an auditory learner. In fact, when I think, I often think in words, whereas most people think in images. Ideas come to me, and I see letters, words, and sentences with very few pictures. Needless to say, when I started thinking about how I wanted to decorate London's room, not many ideas were coming to me, except for one: She would certainly need a canopy.

We finally decided on a little white crib. The back headboard comes up in an arch, and though I normally fawn over mahogany tones, I thought white would be adorable with pink lace and pink sheets. Next we went to the fabric store. I have been in a fabric store on only one other occasion, and it was with my sister. My sister was crocheting for a while, and I admired her skill in doing so. She made lots of beautiful things that she can keep forever, but I never took up knitting myself. I can sew a button on my jeans or fix a hole, but that's as good as it is going to get.

I wanted to find beautiful fabric to use in creating her canopy. I settled on organza, a shiny, shimmery material that seemed very princesslike. When we got home, my husband started assembling the crib, while I watched and took pictures for London's scrapbook. Unlike me, my husband is very artistic and creative. He created a hook out of an old hanger and screwed it into the ceiling. From that hook we hung the fabric, and then pulled the material to the four corners of her crib. When it was finished, and we stepped back and admired the scene, my husband pressed me close to his chest and let a few tears roll down his cheeks. "It looks like an angel lives here," he said.

After all was said and done, and I had crawled into my bed last night, I was so happy that we were ready for London to come home. A huge weight was lifted off my shoulders, as I had heard stories of premature labor. If that happened, I wanted to be ready. The next emotion that came over me was sadness. Her crib is ready, her canopy is up, and her mom and dad are eager to meet her, and yet we have to wait for another month and a half to watch her perfect little body dream in that crib. Suddenly I also started to worry, *What if something awful happens and she never makes it to that crib at all?*

My cousin lost her baby in her eighth month. I felt awful for her, and I couldn't even imagine what it would feel like to lose a dream right before it gets wings. When I heard, my heart ached for her, and yet I don't think it truly hit me what she must have felt until I set up that crib last night. I'm sure my cousin also had a perfect crib filled with the ideas of love and excitement that she had poured into its assembly and creation. I can imagine it is painful to lose a child at any point, but I know, at least for me, it seems it would sting even deeper now that I have prepared a place for her. The thought of her never seeing what Seth and I have done for her in love terrifies me.

God has prepared a place for you. I love how He doesn't just tell us that there is a place we can stay or that we are welcome to join Him in His incredible mansion. But God is truth, and in truth He tells us that not only are there many rooms in His father's house, but that He has gone to prepare one just for you. I'm not sure the gravity of that verse ever struck me so deeply as it has now that I am about to be a mother and have also prepared a place for my child. Enormous amounts of love go into the preparation of a room.

I understand now that in affection, hope, and joy, He has prepared a place just for me, much like I have for London. The only emotion stronger than the excitement He felt in planning and preparing for our arrival is the fear that we'll never come and see what He has done. Unlike me, He is patient. He'll wait as long as it takes, just as long as He gets to see your face light up when you see the work of His hands.

I was asking my husband the other day if he thought I had picked the right Ph.D. program. I had been enrolled in a doctoral program furthering my study of communications. I had even gone to my residency week in Virginia, where I stayed the entire week studying and meeting professors. When I got home, I dropped out. It wasn't that the professors weren't good; they were excellent. It wasn't that the campus wasn't beautiful, because it was. It was that I was there for one week, getting a small taste of what doctoral studies were all about, and in that week I realized I was going to spend the next five or so years eating, sleeping, and breathing communications. I believe that time is short, and that if I am going to be eating, sleeping, and breathing anything, I want it to be religion. So I dropped out of my communications program and entered religious education so that I could study religion more academically, which I haven't done much of in the past.

We were on the couch, and after doing a year's worth of religion electives, I suddenly felt that I was a bit behind where I intended to be at this point in my life.

"Do you think I made a mistake?" I asked him. "I could be done with one year of my doctorate right now, instead of just finishing these electives."

"I'm not sure," he responded. "But I do know that when we go to heaven, you won't be taking a Ph.D. in communications with you. All you will be able to take is your relationship with God, and the relationships you've helped Him make with other people. That's it."

When he said that, I was moved, because I was reminded of what is important. I'm not sure we will have Ph.D.s, doctors, lawyers, or businesspeople in heaven. I am not sure that we will have our BMWs, big houses, or designer clothes. I do know that anything that I do on this earth to better prepare me for His kingdom, those efforts I can take with me. He has gone to prepare a place for me, and so He needs me to show up. He has also gone to prepare a place for the person next to me, but what if I were the person that was supposed to explain to them how to get there safely, but, for whatever shortcoming, I didn't? What if because of what I didn't do, they miss their exit?

I am sure that the first moment I see my daughter will be powerful, but in honesty, the moment I look forward to most is when I get to take her home and walk her inside the room I have prepared solely for her. All I can do in the meantime is pray that God will allow me that opportunity to take her home. And it's been only now, in the midst of these prayers, that God has shown me that I am not the only one standing around anxious. He too is anxious, desperate to take us home to the rooms that by His sweat and nail-scarred hands He has prepared, intimately, lovingly, and individually. Now, I don't know if there will be a canopy, but I am certain that either way, it will be a room fit for an angel.

Reflection: "'My Father's house has many rooms; if that were not so, would I have told you that I am going there to prepare a place for you? And if I go and prepare a place for you, I will come back and take you to be with me that you also may be where I am. You know the way to the place where I am going.' Thomas said to him, 'Lord, we don't know where you are going, so how can we know the way?' Jesus answered, 'I am the way and the truth and the life. No one comes to the Father except through me. If you really know me, you will know my Father as well. From now on, you do know him and have seen him'" (John 14:2-7).

Day 29

"It's often just enough to be with someone.
I don't need to touch them. Not even talk.
A feeling passes between you both. You're not alone."

—Marilyn Monroe

A student in my English class this week told a very heartwarming story about himself. It was the first day of classes, and I typically ask the students to write down an introduction for themselves, something that you may see on their social network that tells a bit about what has made them who they are. Then I ask them to share these with the class, and that is how we get to know one another.

One student read his, and it wasn't the typical Q&A I was used to hearing. Usually they say where they were born, what is important to them, what they do for a living, general things that create further conversation but that don't really reveal too much about their personal lives. This student, however, left us silent.

He said that his life had started over a few years ago. He had been driving home on leave from the military when his car had crashed with a motorcyclist. The cyclist had been killed instantly, and for a long time my student had also endured his own sort of funeral. He had become severely depressed by the incident, and after a few months had been honorably discharged from the military. The loss of another man's life because of his driving, though it had been found not to be his fault, had still eaten him alive. Life had lost meaning, and the more he had learned about the man who had died, the more guilt had devoured him. He said that he had always been a man of faith, but that this unexpected turn of events had brought him to his darkest hour.

Then he explained that last year a sudden break in the clouds had appeared. He had contacted the family of the motorcyclist, and they had agreed to allow him into their home to visit. He had met with them for a weekend, and said that the compassion and love that they had shown him had been unlike any other display of kindness he had ever seen before. They told him about the man they had lost, and encouraged him to find peace, because they had. Those days with that family had changed the rest of his life, and he was now back in school, living again, and hoping for an opportunity to show someone else the same love that this broken family had shown to him.

His story sat heavy on my heart because it proved to me again that often the greatest acts in life are those done out of kindness. I think, far too often, we compare ourselves to one another. We think, *There are so many talented people in this world, and I am not one of them; surely God can't use me,* and so we do nothing. This man's life was not changed by a sermon, or my book, or a song written by a top-selling record label. His life was changed when, in his darkest hour, someone loved him through it.

I found a poem that I had written on May 9, 2003. Several students in my high school had died recently, and it was a strange state that the students were living in. I had written this poem then, and I want to share it with you now, if you don't mind a little advice from a 16-year-old kid.

Love can extend
The lives that may end,
Or the sadness that grows with the year.
And love can mend
The hearts that bend,
And whisper to the lonely ear.
Love can trace
The laughter erased,
And sketch a smile, too.
Love can create
Where your heart once ached,
And make fond memories new.
When sorrow and grief
And all else you weep
Turns a heart once warm to stone;
When times of trial
Tear through your smile
And leave you feeling alone,
Call on the Lord;
Let prayer be your sword,
And face all your demons head-on.
Let faith escape
A heart that did break,

And let love hold the soul that's now gone.
But love can do nothing
If you don't do something
To share it with somebody else.
It takes a friend
To teach love again.
So let love—
Be love—
And help.

On Day 29 of our walk together, I pray that you will share the one gift everyone has within them—love—and give it away. At the end of the day, whether you play the guitar or can barely sing in the shower, our biggest ministry should simply be loving people right here in everyday life. Connecting with God is about letting Him live inside of you. It's about connecting with His people and discussing matters bigger than reality television.

There has never been a generation more apt to handling a lack of face-to-face communication than this one is, and yet it seems God is the only friend we can't seem to find time to connect with. Still, our friends list is full of people we text, but do not see; tweet, but do not see; and post, but do not see. We make time for those virtual friendships, and yet feel inconvenienced in building a relationship with a God we cannot see. You'd think that this mediavore generation would be ready to connect through communication that does not require face-to-face interaction in order to be gratifying, and yet are we?

Here's the thing, the catch that once you discover, you'll never be able to put God down. We may not be blessed with the ability to see Christ face to face, but He does allow us to feel Him, and once you are touched by a spirit that powerful, your whole world becomes kinesthetic. So just let love—be love—and help.

Reflection: "And I will ask the Father, and he will give you another advocate to help and be with you forever—the Spirit of truth. The world cannot accept him, because it neither sees him nor knows him. But you know him, for he lives with you and will be in you" (John 14:16, 17).

Day 30

"We cannot do great things on this earth,
only small things with great love."
—Mother Teresa

Sometimes the only thing more powerful than the words we've said are the ones that we didn't. Sometimes we meet people, people who don't just fade into the background. Maybe it's someone you don't really talk to but you've noticed, or someone whom you do know well and you just can't seem to find the right words to let them know that, for whatever reason, they are pressed to your heart.

I meet a lot of people each semester through teaching. In a typical semester I will meet 100 new students. That's 100 names to learn, papers to grade, faces to match to my roster when hands are raised; but it's also 100 souls.

I have said it before, but I do not work in a Christian institution, and because of this I sincerely view my job as a ministry. I don't teach courses about math and history, so I am not bogged down by dates and figures. I teach courses that deal with people and the way we produce and create messages to send to one another. I know that many of the professors I work with are excellent teachers. I know because my students tell me. These professors are good at winning the battle of keeping their classes' attention. To do this, many professors have to resort to all sorts of zingers and one-liners that may be nestled up their sleeves. Everyone knows that sex sells, so working that into your lecture somehow is a surefire way to keep them with you. Indecent jokes, curse words, saying the unexpected—it's all part of the fight to keep from losing them.

I don't rely on these tactics. Instead, I ask God to enter the classroom with me, and I have to represent Him without mentioning His name. Not only am I mindful of the things I say, I also have to pay attention to the way that I make them feel, and so I spend a lot of hours preparing my lectures and thinking of ways to keep their attention.

I quickly saw that many people do not have loving mothers and fathers or friends who are telling them that they can do anything, and so I put a lot of time and sweat and prayer into hoping that I can make them feel special, that they deserve an education and have a real chance at succeeding in whatever they do. Doing this and not coming across cheesy or boring is not easy. It's like being a comedian: throw a few raunchy jokes and the crowd loves you, but making them laugh while keeping it clean is not as simple as one might think.

It is not just my love for words but also my study of communication theory and practice that has taught me just how much of an impact our messages have on one another. Change your words, and you can literally change your world. I try to teach this concept to my students. That much of communication is purposeful, and once we really allow that thought to resonate, it should change the way we produce messages. If what you say is said with an agenda, how should that affect the words that come out of your mouth?

C. H. Cooley has a communications theory called the looking-glass self, which essentially says that we build our self-perception based off of what others tell us we are. He said, "Each to each a looking-glass, reflects the other that doth pass." We perceive what others might think of our appearance, our character, our intelligence, our aims or motives, and from that we gain our identity. If this is true, and I think that often it is, then what application does it have for us as Christians?

Cooley also said, "I am not what I think I am and I am not what you think I am; I am what I think that you think I am." In my mind, this means that the words we say and the words we don't say are extremely powerful. Whether you tell me I'm dumb, or you simply never tell me you think I am smart, you are sending me a message, and I am using that as I form my identity.

I often ask my students the question "If communication is such an important and vital part of the human experience, why do you think many of us don't bother to study it academically?" Their response is usually the same, that since we talk to people every day, we all assume we already understand how communication works, and therefore do not bother to learn about it. In my opinion, it should be that *because* we use it every day, we should all take the time to learn about it. I think this goes for everyone, but I think it should especially ring true for Christians, people who believe that God is using them as tools for various tasks when dealing with His people.

Christ dedicated His life on earth to using His messages wisely to create a response in the hearts of people, and as His followers, shouldn't we be doing the same? The words that you say are powerful, but perhaps more powerful are the ones you didn't say. These are the moments that passed you by in which you could have made a difference but didn't. We can't just want to connect with God; we have to want to connect with God so that He can fill our hearts as we connect with other people. The second you fall in love with God, your very next step should be to share Him with someone else. If you have never done that, no matter how good you are, you are missing the most crucial part of the Christian experience.

I had a class the other morning in which my professor posed two questions: 1. How successful has Satan been in preventing the truth of God's message? 2. What is your responsibility regarding that truth?

If there are two points I can have you take away from our 30 days together it is that you must first connect with God yourself and then you must share Him with someone else. You cannot share Christ with others without first connecting with Him yourself, because you'll be doing more damage than good. My husband always says, "Many Christians know just enough of God to be dangerous." He means that we know more than someone who knows nothing, but when we share we do it through hate, not love, and so we have only hurt the cause. Likewise, you cannot connect with God and then remain silent. Love is like fire; it's contagious. If it's not consuming everything you touch, you probably aren't in it. Remember that a characteristic of our generation is that we are mediavores. We are stuffed full of social networking Web sites, reality television, gaming entertainment, and cinematic productions. We consume media and tabloids at rates like never before. We are already full, and yet I am asking you to go out and start feeding yourself spiritually.

Get involved in community and devour the Word of God with a small group or Bible study. He is preparing you for His return, but the time is coming when the announcement will ring and Revelation 22:11 will be fulfilled. "Let the one who does wrong continue to do wrong; let the vile person continue to be vile; let the one who does right continue to do right; and let the holy person continue to be holy."

I hope the past 30 days we've spent together have made you hungry for more. Don't put this book on your shelf feeling good because you have another devotional you can talk about when someone asks you a worship thought; keep devouring. Study the Scriptures, read other work, spend time in prayer, and tell God that you are desperate to connect yourself with Him. We are approaching the final stage, and you simply don't have time to be stagnant.

We are now living in a wireless generation. Never before has communication literally had the ability to reach globally as it has now. A little 5-year-old boy smokes a cigarette in Asia, and within days he is a YouTube sensation in America.

The Bible tells us in Matthew 24:14, "And this gospel of the kingdom will be preached in the whole world as a testimony to all nations, and then the end will come." Christ is coming; our tech-savvy culture is making sure of that, and you can help prepare the way for Him. The next time you're about to post statuses with the latest YouTube hit or leave a reality television show reference on your Twitter account, think about those two questions my professor posed: How successful has Satan been in preventing the truth of God's message, and what is your responsibility regarding that truth?

You are fooling yourself if you think you do not have a responsibility in aiding Christ to prepare His people. There is present truth to be shared, and you have a duty to be sharing it. Share with them your love, share with them your Savior, share with them your good news, and if Ellen White is right in her end-of-times teachings (which I have full confidence that she is), you must figure out how to share with them your Sabbath. If Satan has been successful in preventing the truth of God's message, whom can we blame but ourselves? And what is your current responsibility regarding that truth?

Have you ever just felt something so powerfully in your gut that you just experienced some internal animal-like instinct that just really urged you on something? That is how I am feeling about God's return. I feel Him gnawing at my heart and soul, that the time is near and He needs His people to move. This train is going with or without you, but you know how God is: He's desperate to see you join in. He's been holding back the tides for you and me, but He can't keep holding much longer. He has children in other countries and areas that are begging for Him to intercede, and so even though He wants to give more time to every bending heart, He has to move. He can't stand the sight of death, pain, and despair any longer, and so the time is coming for Him to allow the final stage to be set and allow Satan to roam. He's raising up a generation of young people to lead His cause, and I am wondering what your personal responsibility is in all of this.

You have a responsibility to use your words to change this world.

Hopefully, if my prayers have been answered, you've just spent the past 30 days connecting with Jesus Christ, and now the only thing left to do is to let what you've learned go viral.

Reflection: "For the Son of Man is going to come in his Father's glory with his angels, and then he will reward each person according to what they have done" (Matthew 16:27).

Heather Thinks You're Ready for Some Good News

Cracked Glasses

Heather Thompson Day

Heather Thompson Day has some good news for those of us who think we've made too many mistakes. Sure, we have good intentions. But usually they lie shattered at our feet. What value could we possibly be to God in this condition? We're ruined. Useless.

In her newest book she explores myths that make us feel we're not good enough for God. She also points out those distractions that keep us from connecting with Him at a deeper level.

Heather is open about being a cracked glass herself. No real Christian is perfect, you know— just repaired. Regularly. 978-0-8280-2564-5